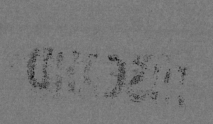

WHICH SIDE ARE YOU ON?

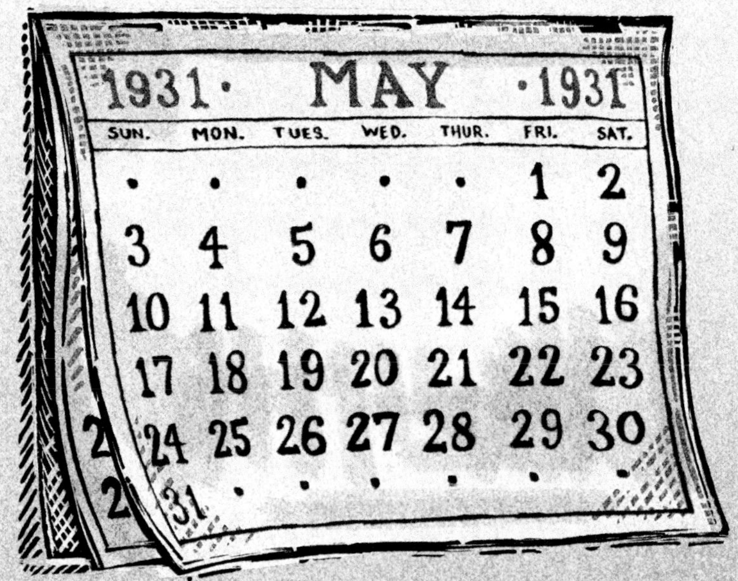
1931 · MAY · 1931
SUN. MON. TUES. WED. THUR. FRI. SAT.
1 2
3 4 5 6 7 8 9
10 11 12 13 14 15 16
17 18 19 20 21 22 23
24 25 26 27 28 29 30
31

The story of a song

BY GEORGE ELLA LYON
ARTWORK BY CHRISTOPHER CARDINALE

IN MEMORY OF
FLORENCE REECE
(1900-1986)
&
HAZEL DICKENS
(1935-2011)

For the people of Harlan County
and for all who sing out for justice,
especially Jean Ritchie,
the Reel World String Band,
Jessie Lynne, Jason, Silas, Anne, & Kate

—G.E.L.

For the workers, organizers, their families, and friends
who have taken a stand to protect our right
to labor and live with dignity

For my son, Macéo,
who will inherit the fruits of this struggle

—C.C.

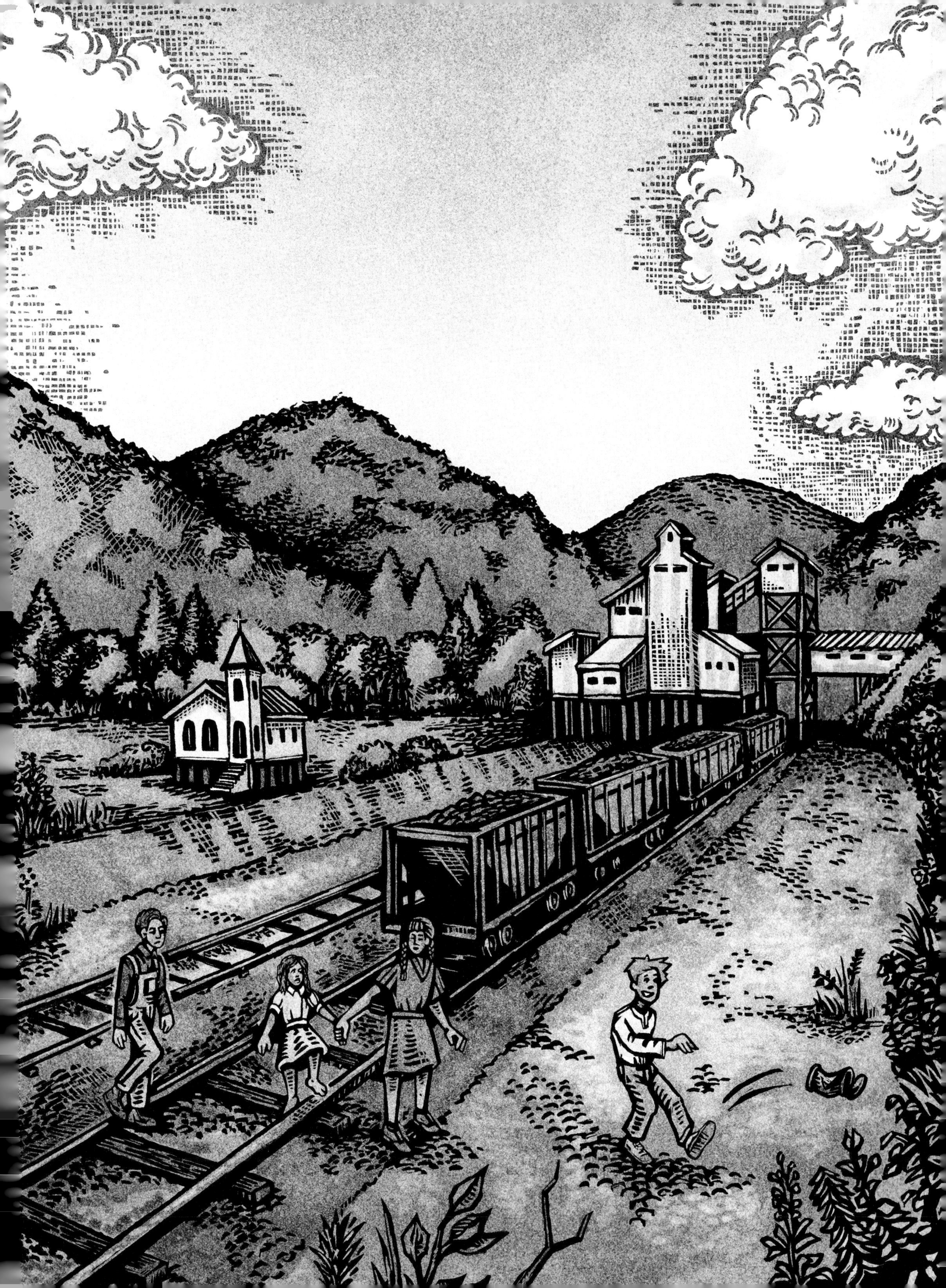

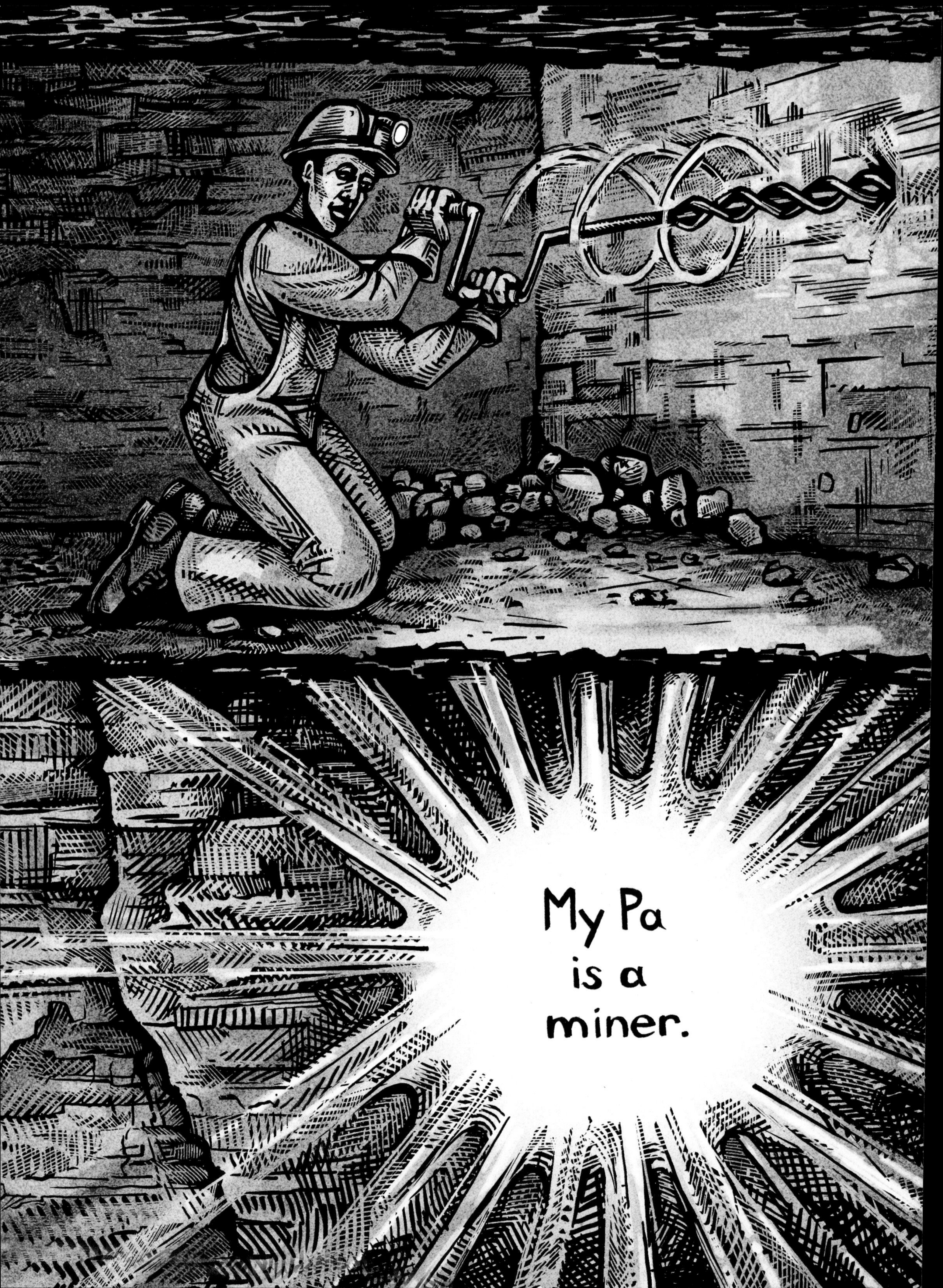
My Pa
is a
miner.

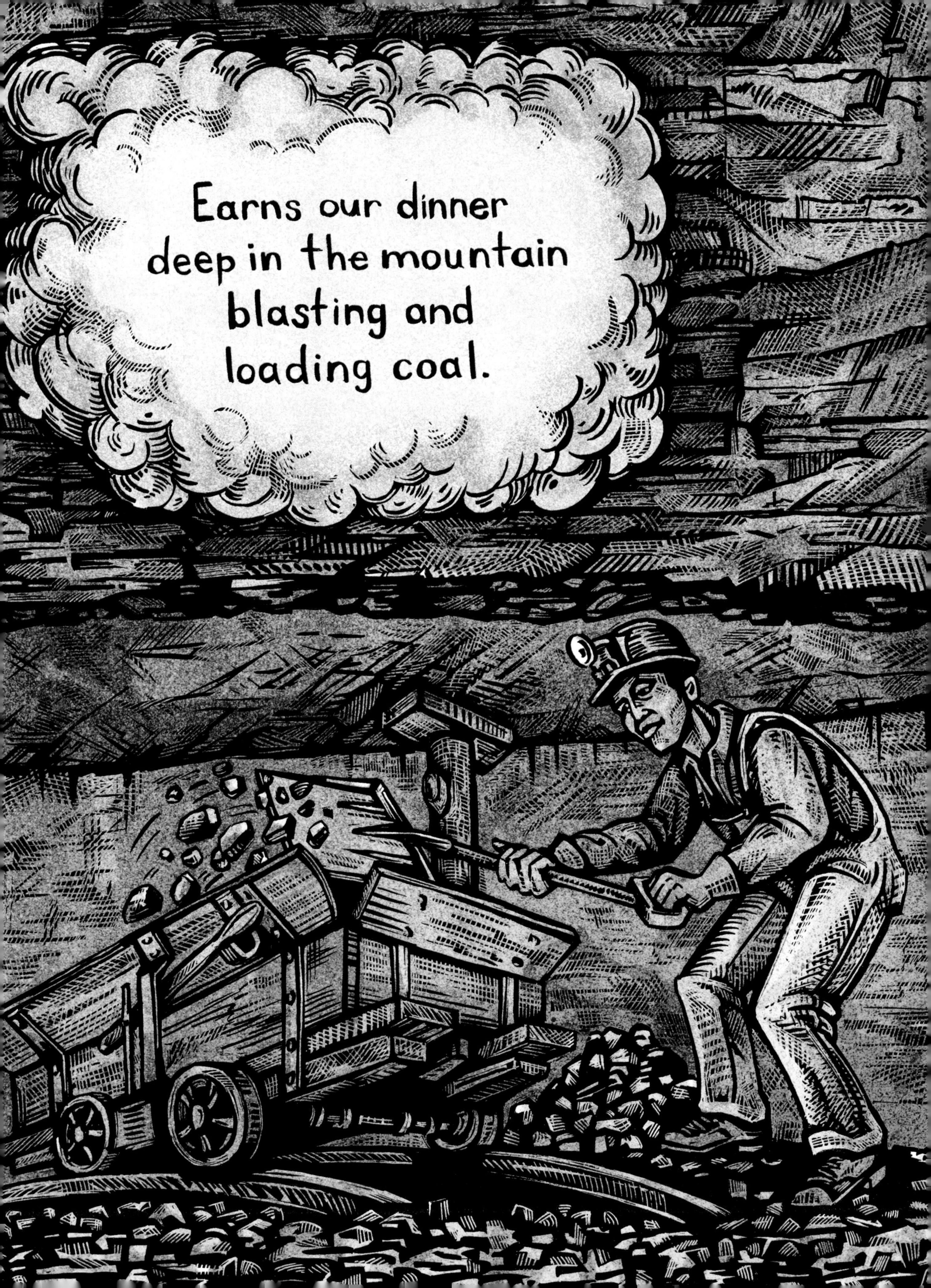
Earns our dinner
deep in the mountain
blasting and
loading coal.

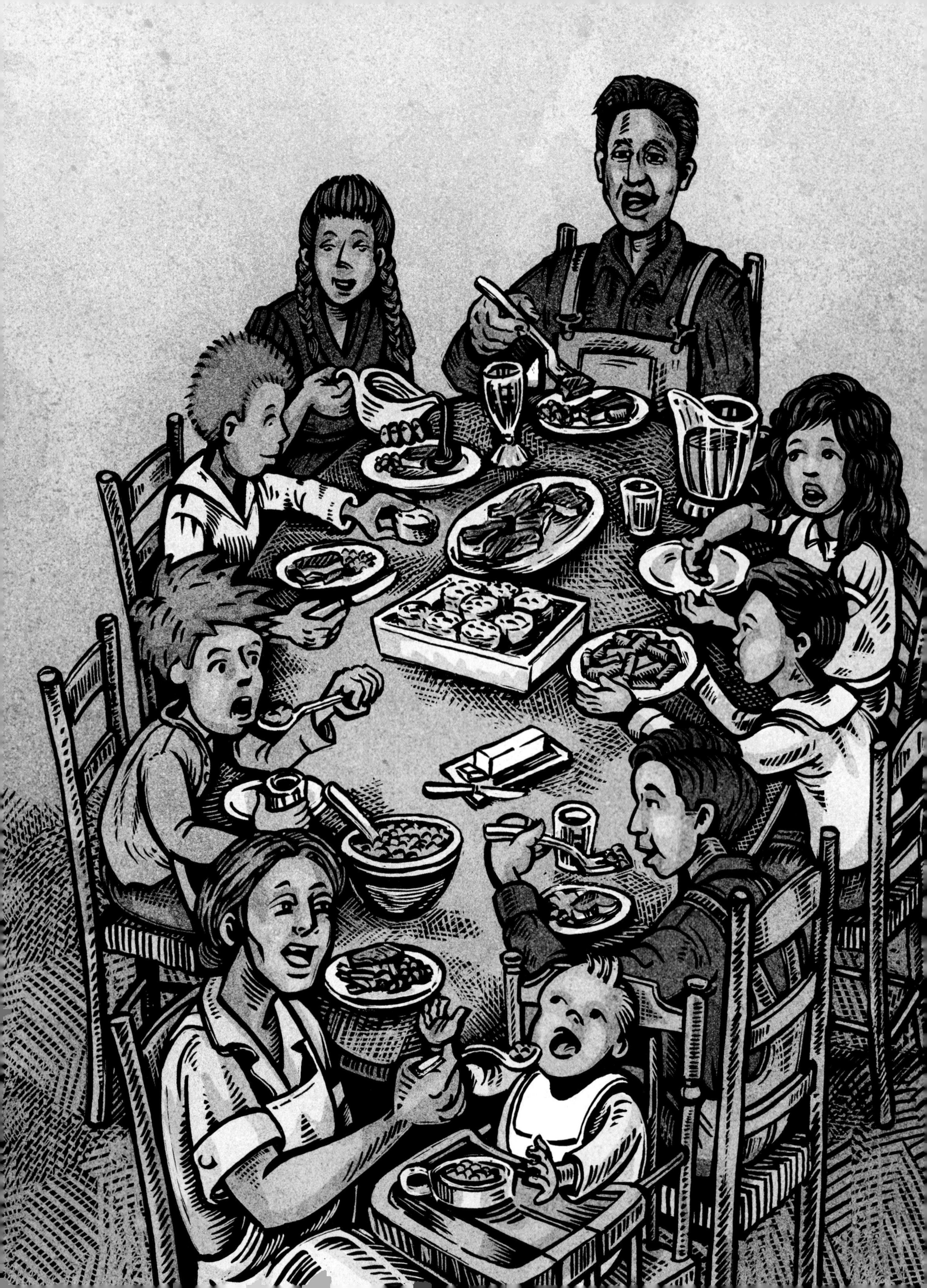

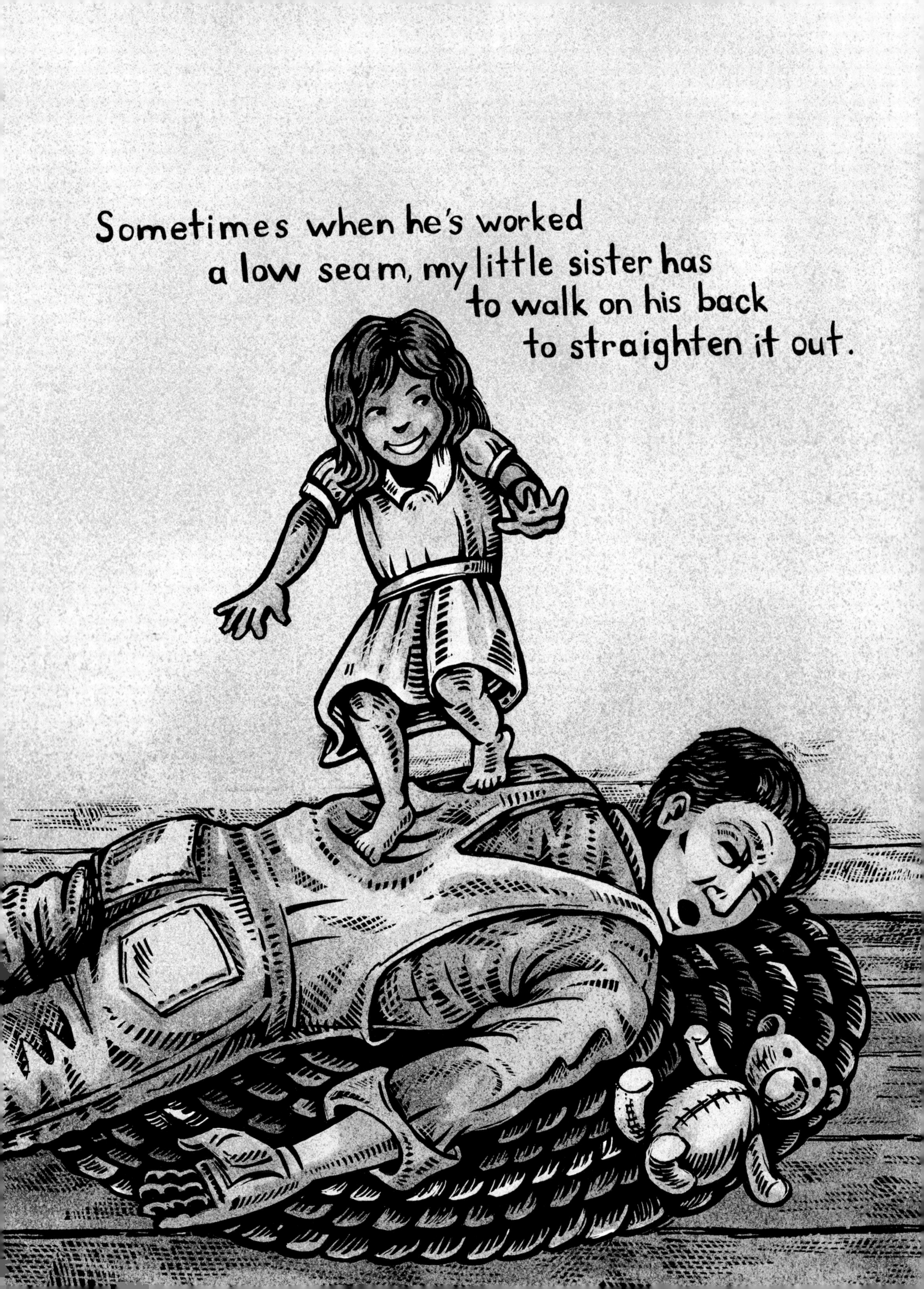
Sometimes when he's worked a low seam, my little sister has to walk on his back to straighten it out.

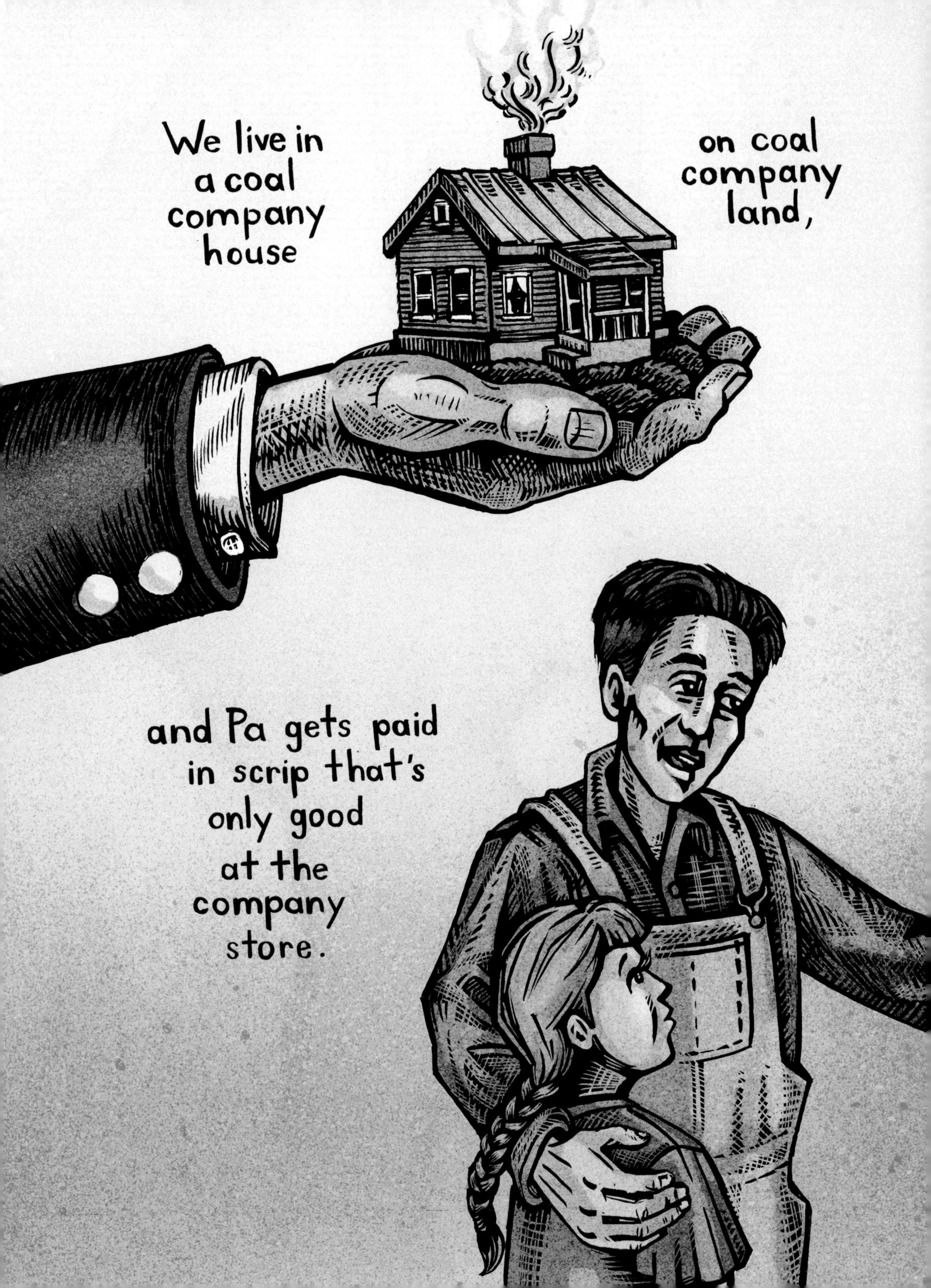
We live in a coal company house
on coal company land,
and Pa gets paid in scrip that's only good at the company store.

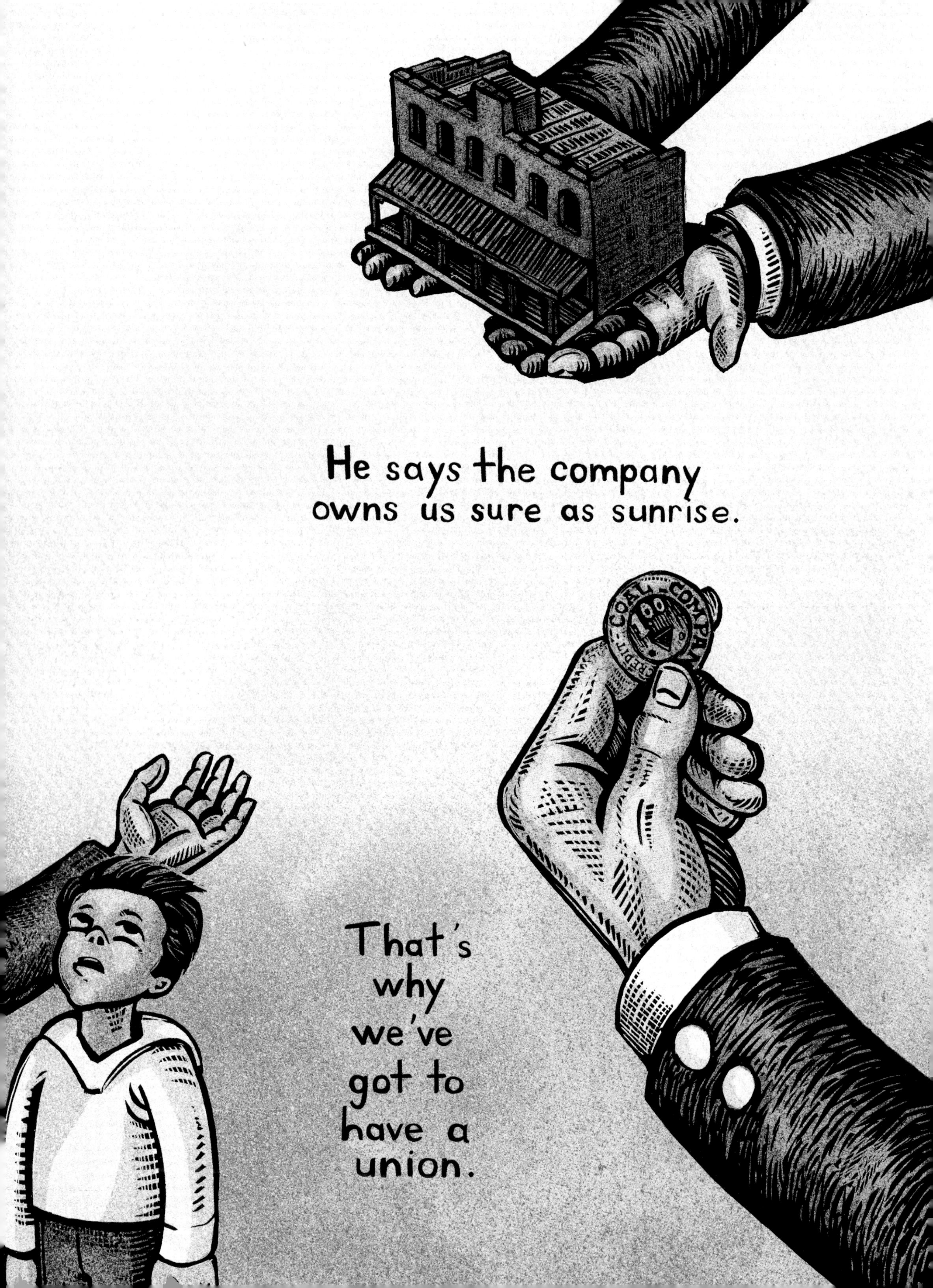
He says the company owns us sure as sunrise.
That's why we've got to have a union.

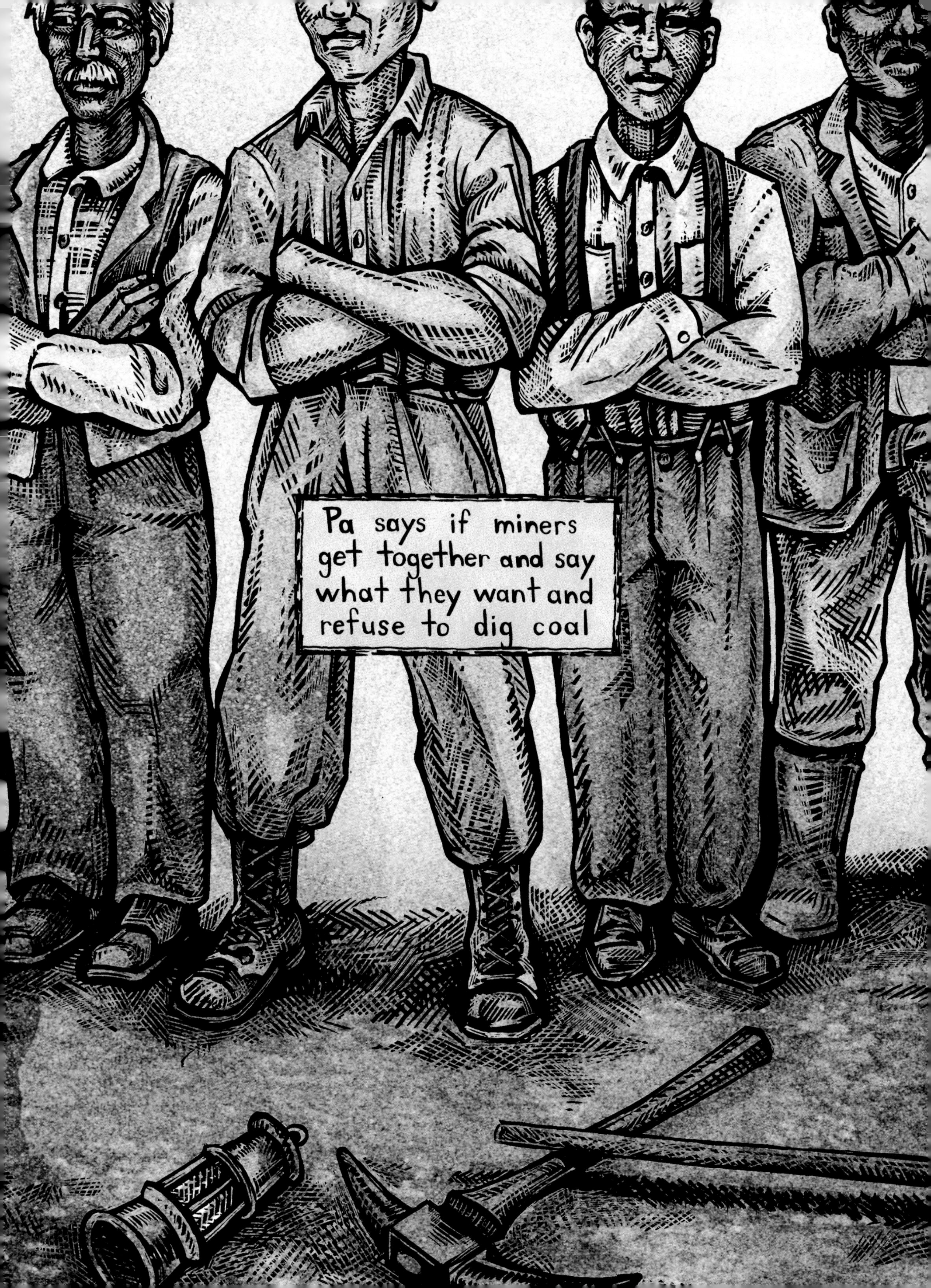
Pa says if miners get together and say what they want and refuse to dig coal

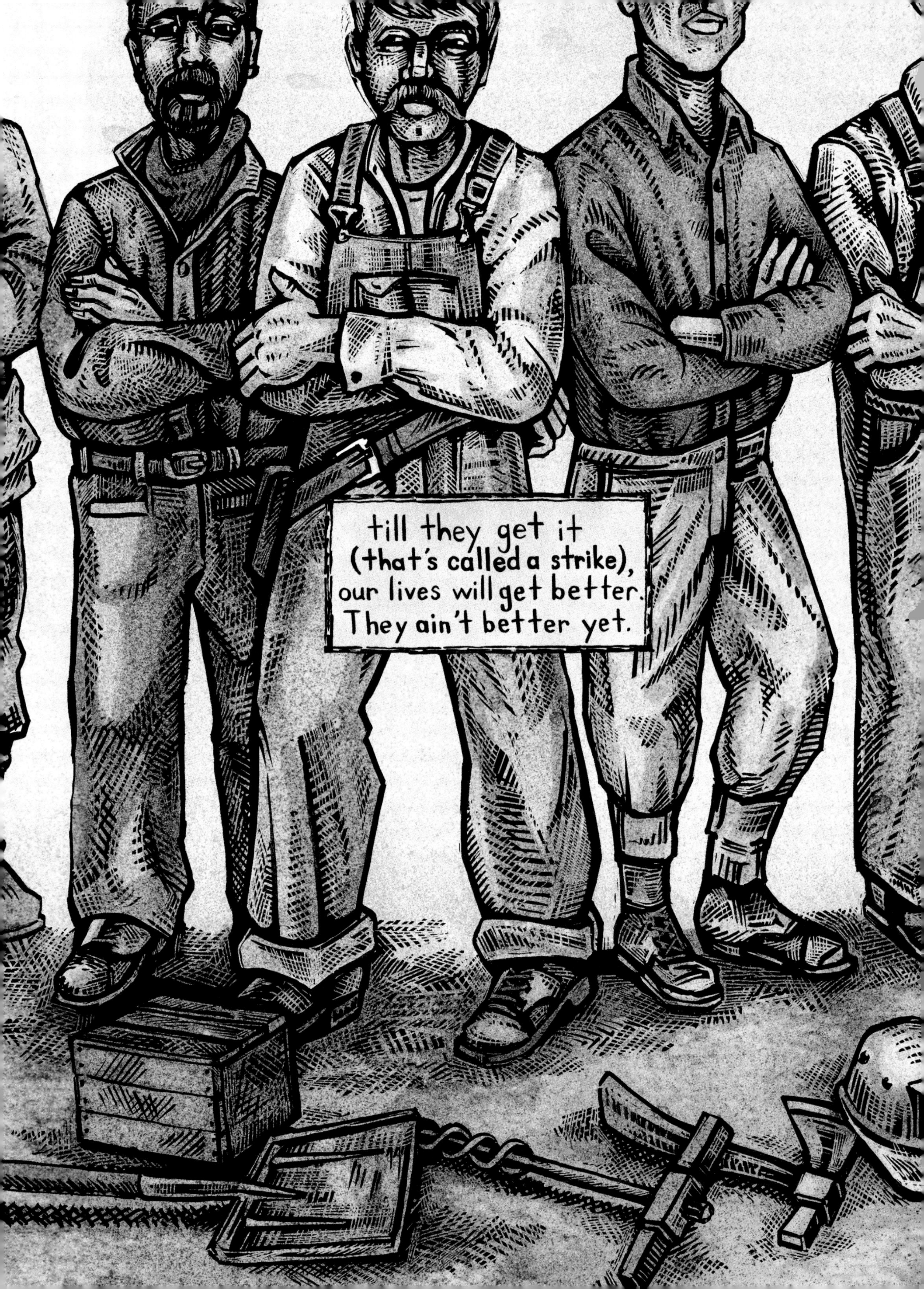
till they get it (that's called a strike), our lives will get better. They ain't better yet.

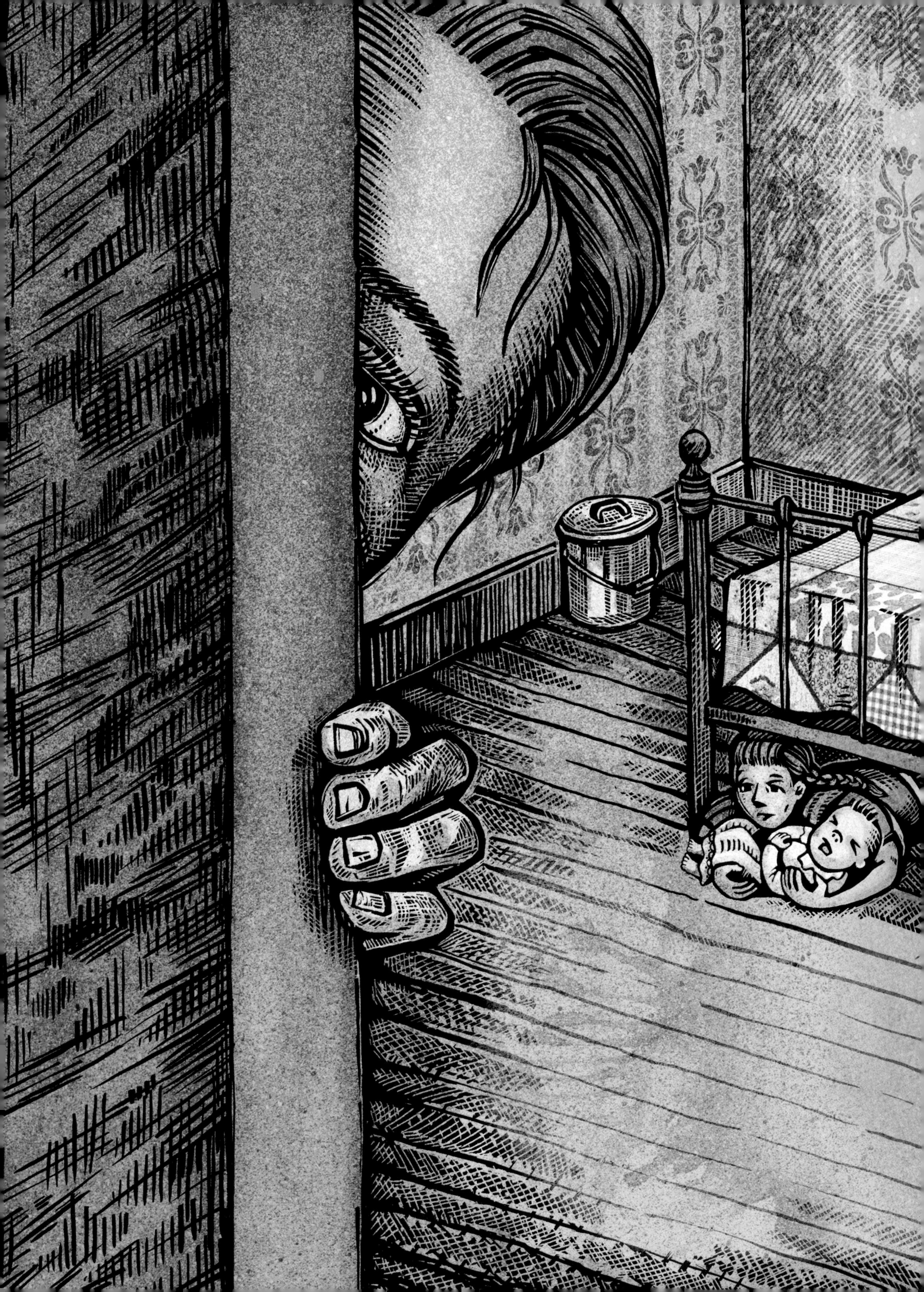

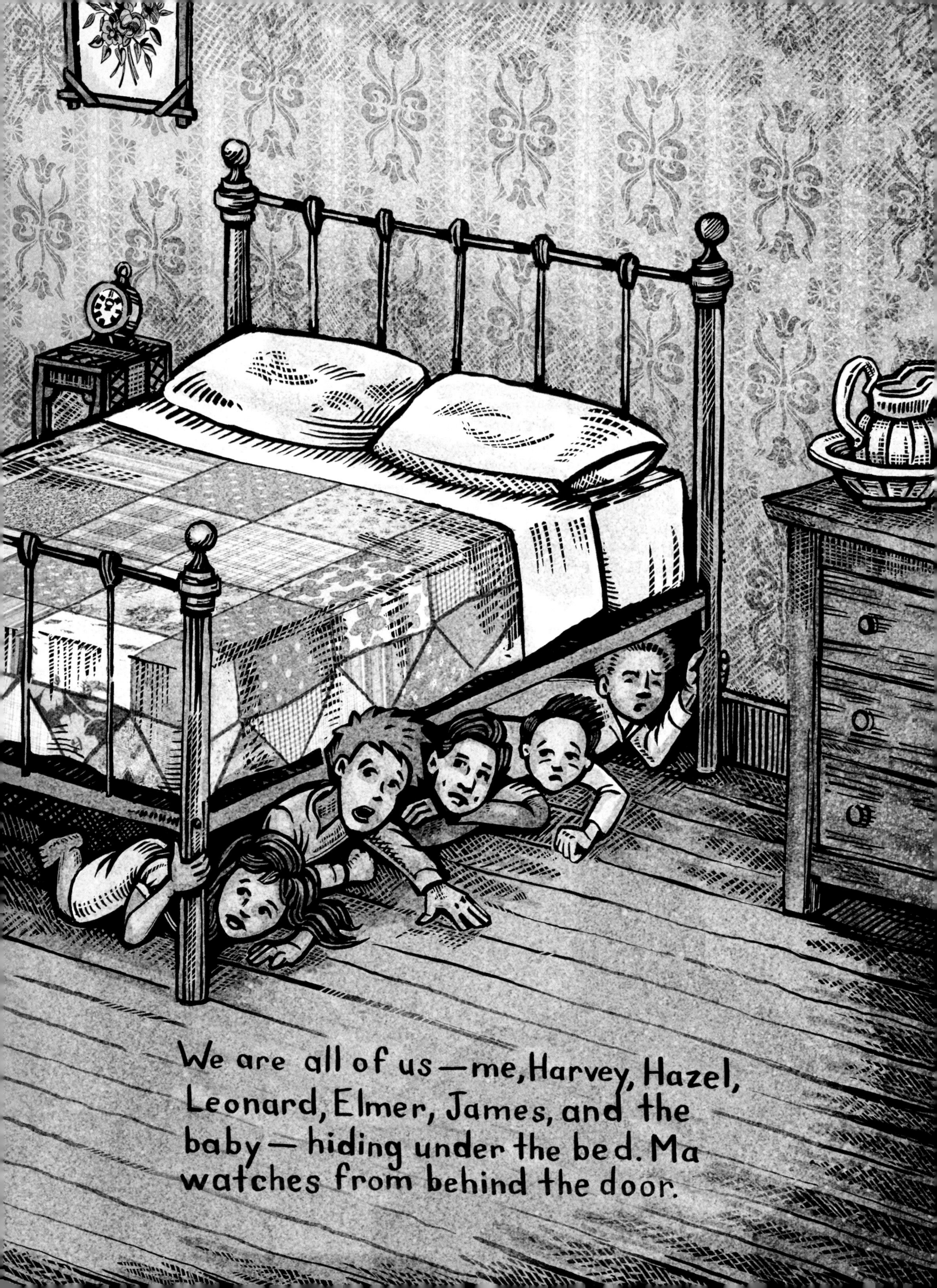

We are all of us—me, Harvey, Hazel, Leonard, Elmer, James, and the baby—hiding under the bed. Ma watches from behind the door.

Not hiding
from a
storm

or a bear
that's got
into this
holler.

Not
from
a
thief.

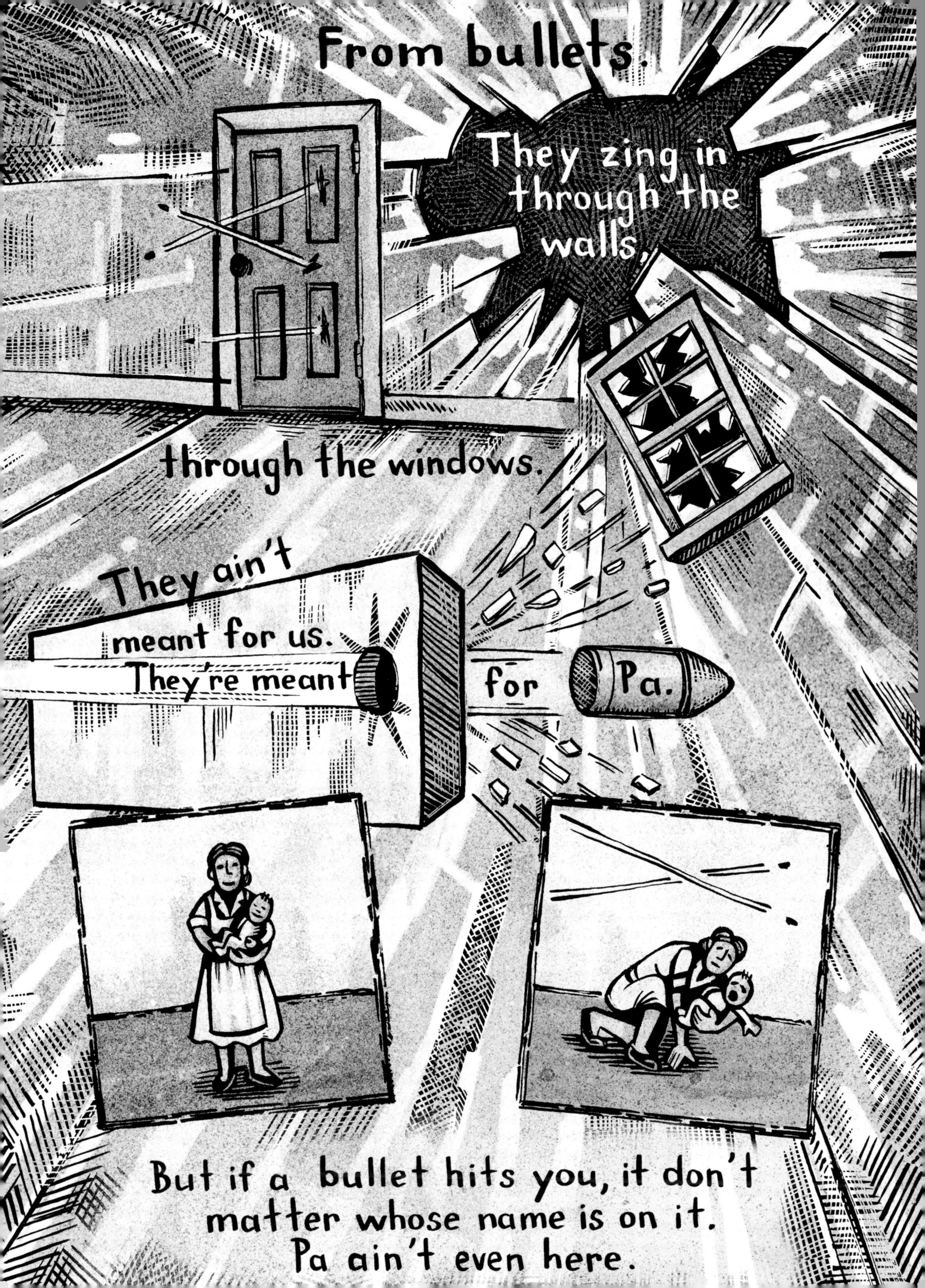
From bullets.
They zing in through the walls,
through the windows.
They ain't meant for us.
They're meant for Pa.
But if a bullet hits you, it don't matter whose name is on it.
Pa ain't even here.

Ma heard that Sheriff Blair
was sending gun thugs after Pa.

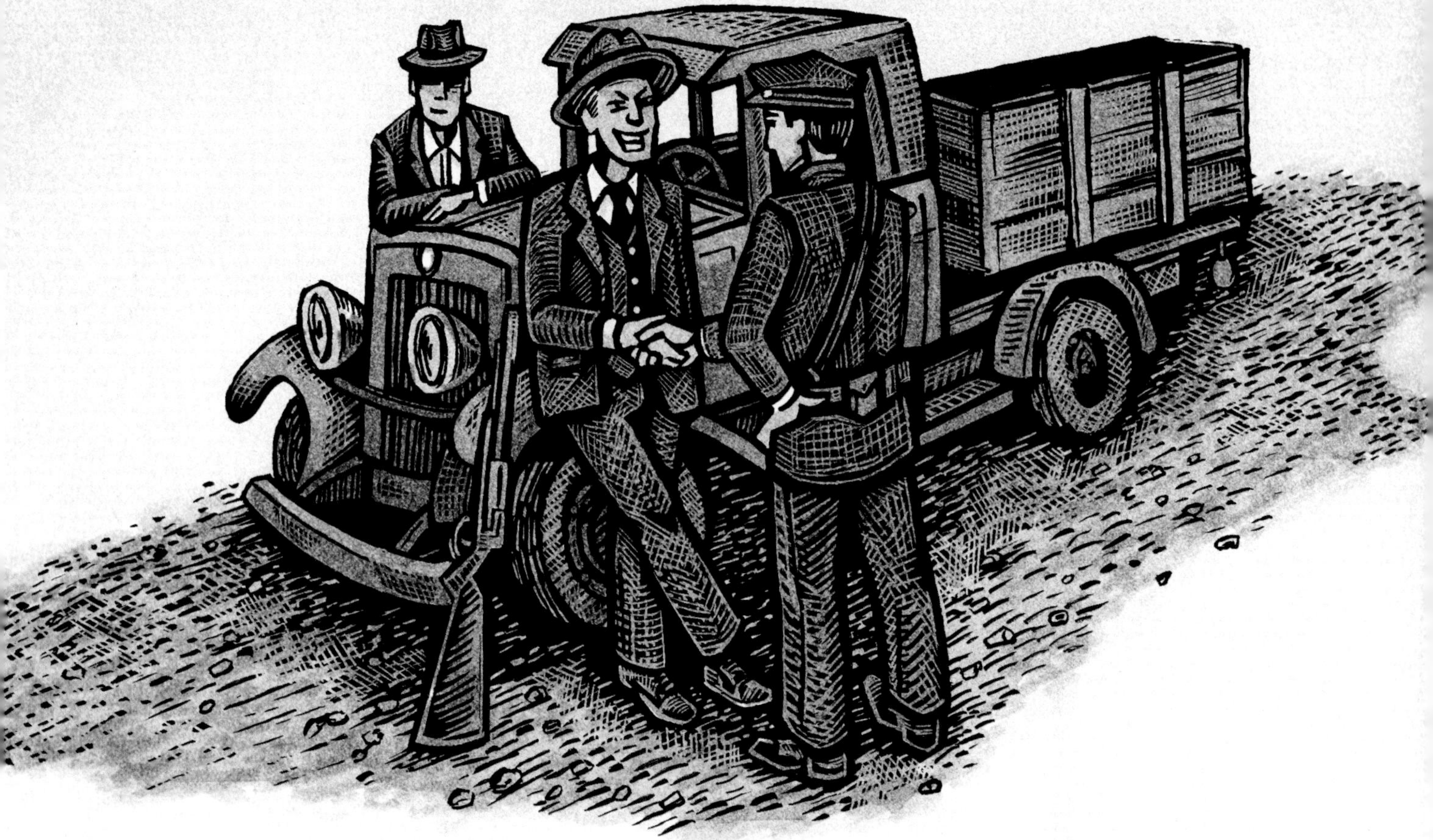

She got word to him not to come home, and he
lit out over the mountain.

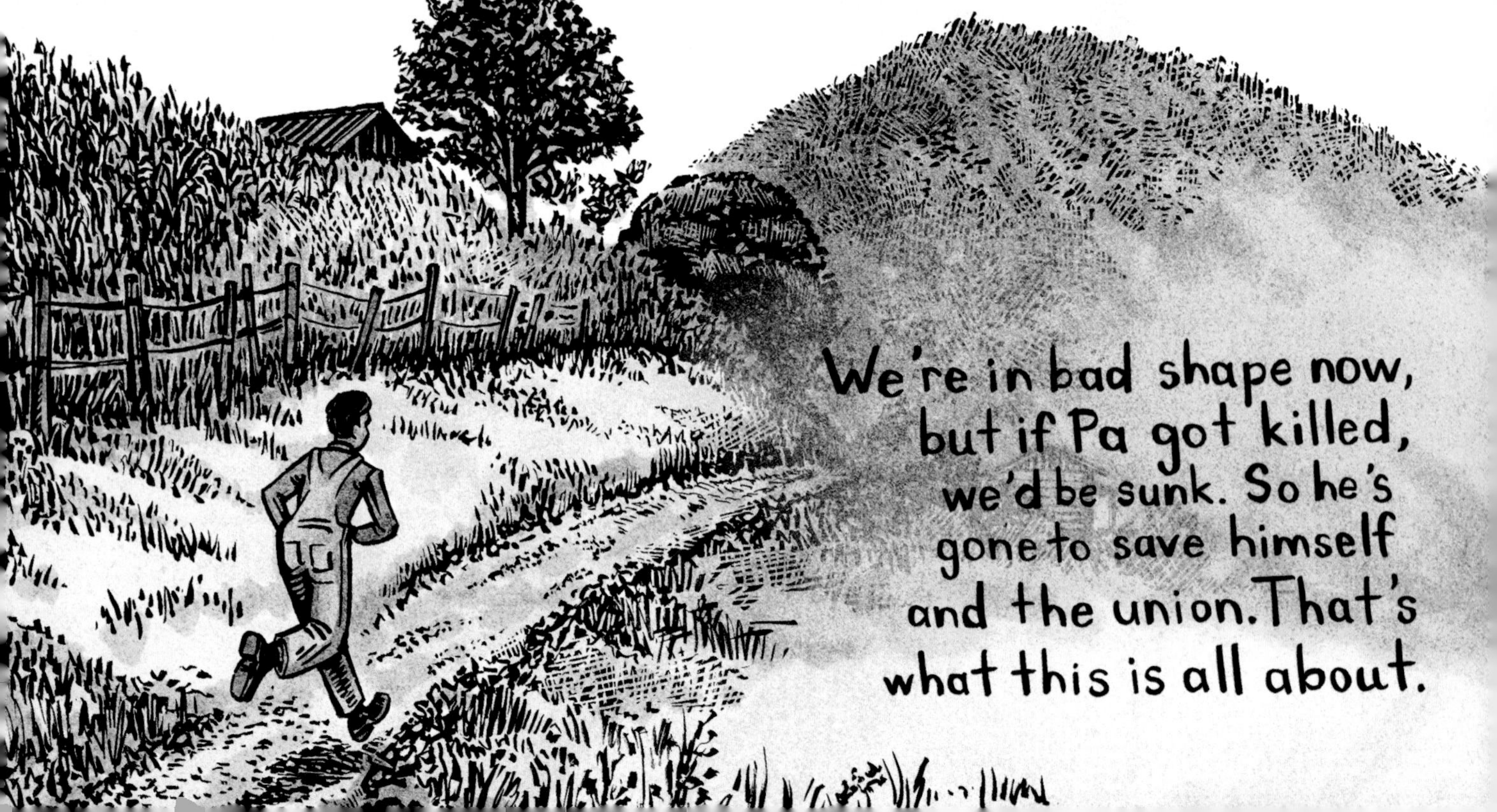
We're in bad shape now, but if Pa got killed, we'd be sunk. So he's gone to save himself and the union. That's what this is all about.

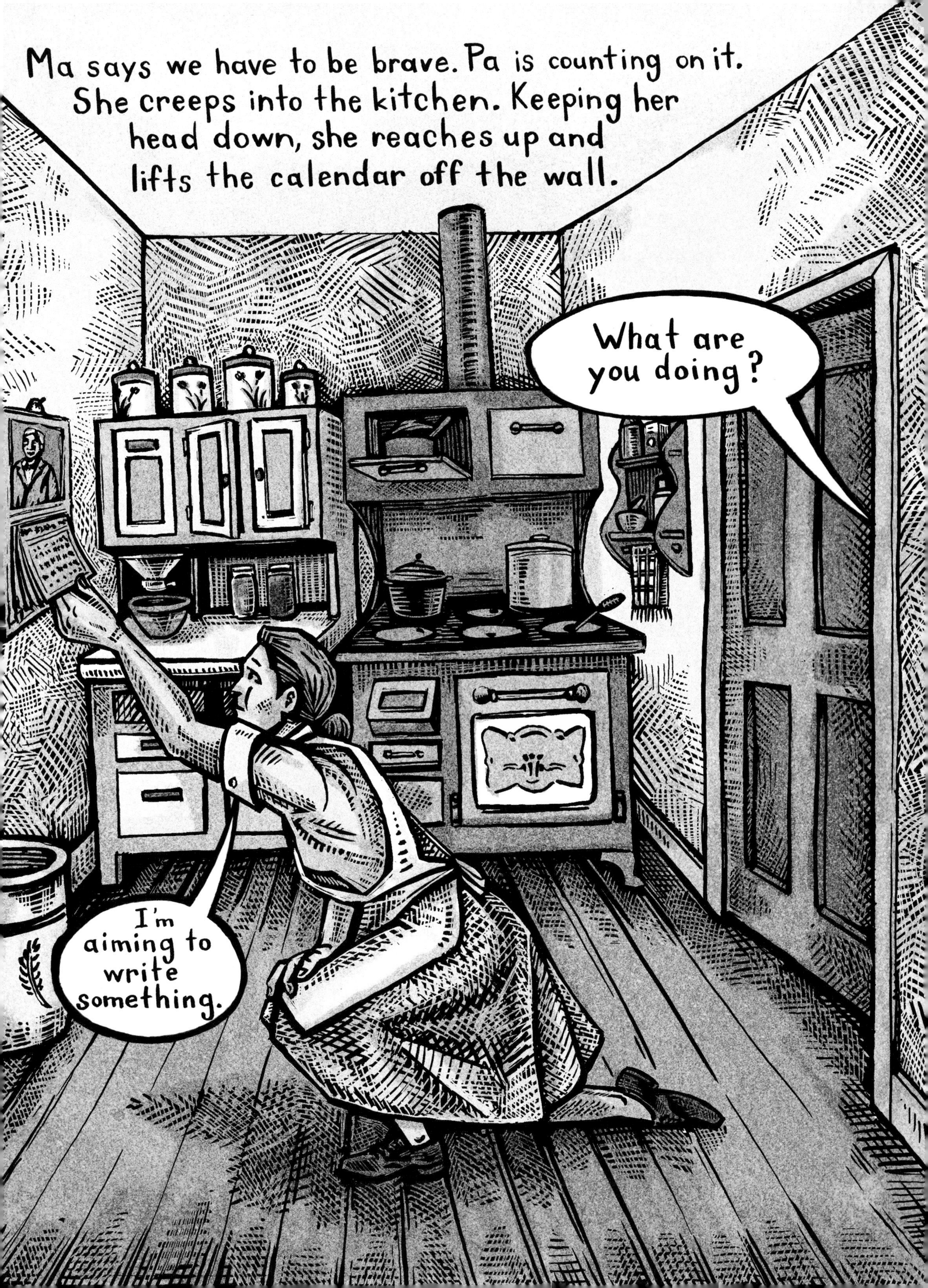
Ma says we have to be brave. Pa is counting on it. She creeps into the kitchen. Keeping her head down, she reaches up and lifts the calendar off the wall.
What are you doing?
I'm aiming to write something.

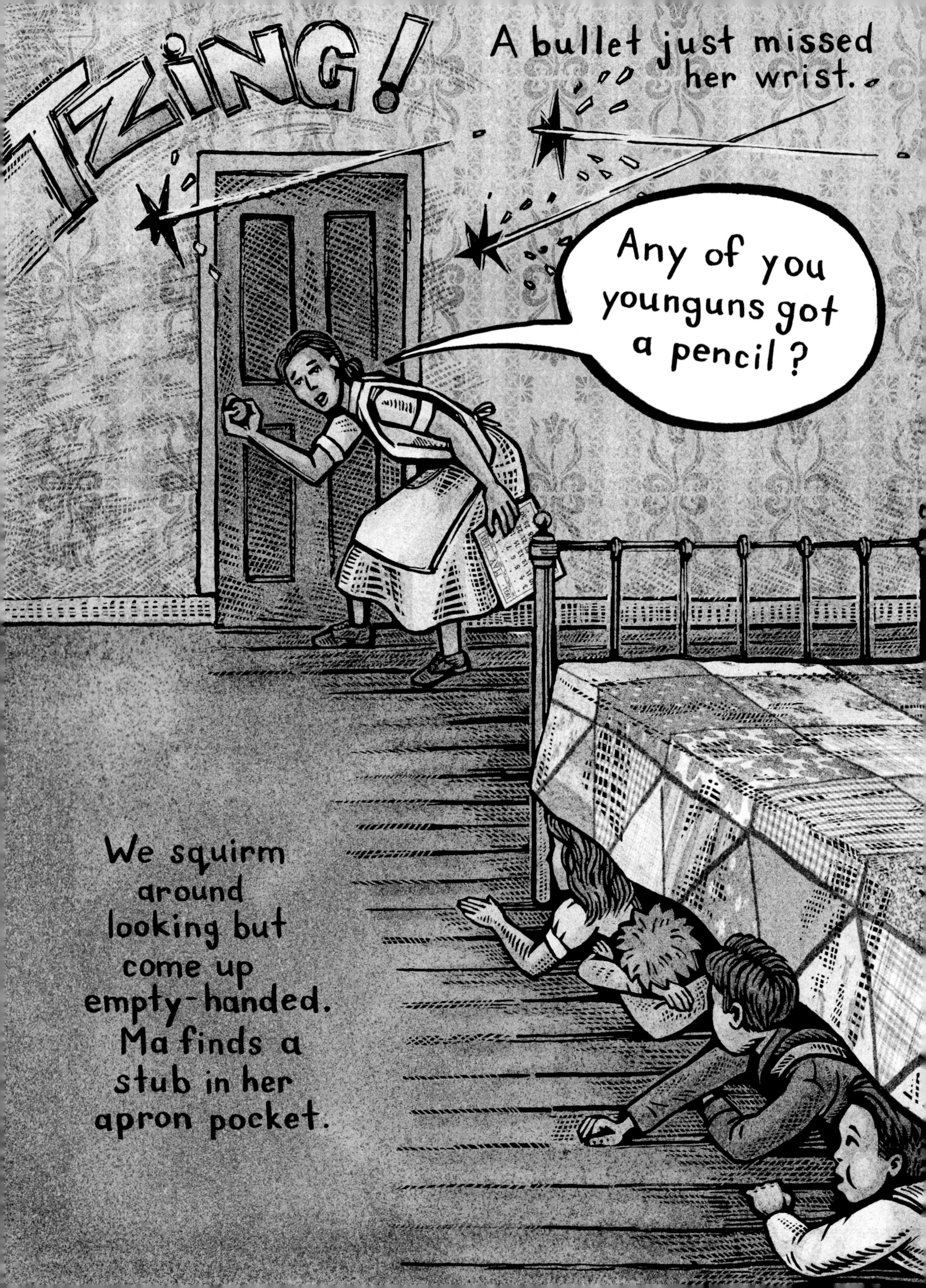
TZING!
A bullet just missed her wrist.
Any of you younguns got a pencil?
We squirm around looking but come up empty-handed. Ma finds a stub in her apron pocket.

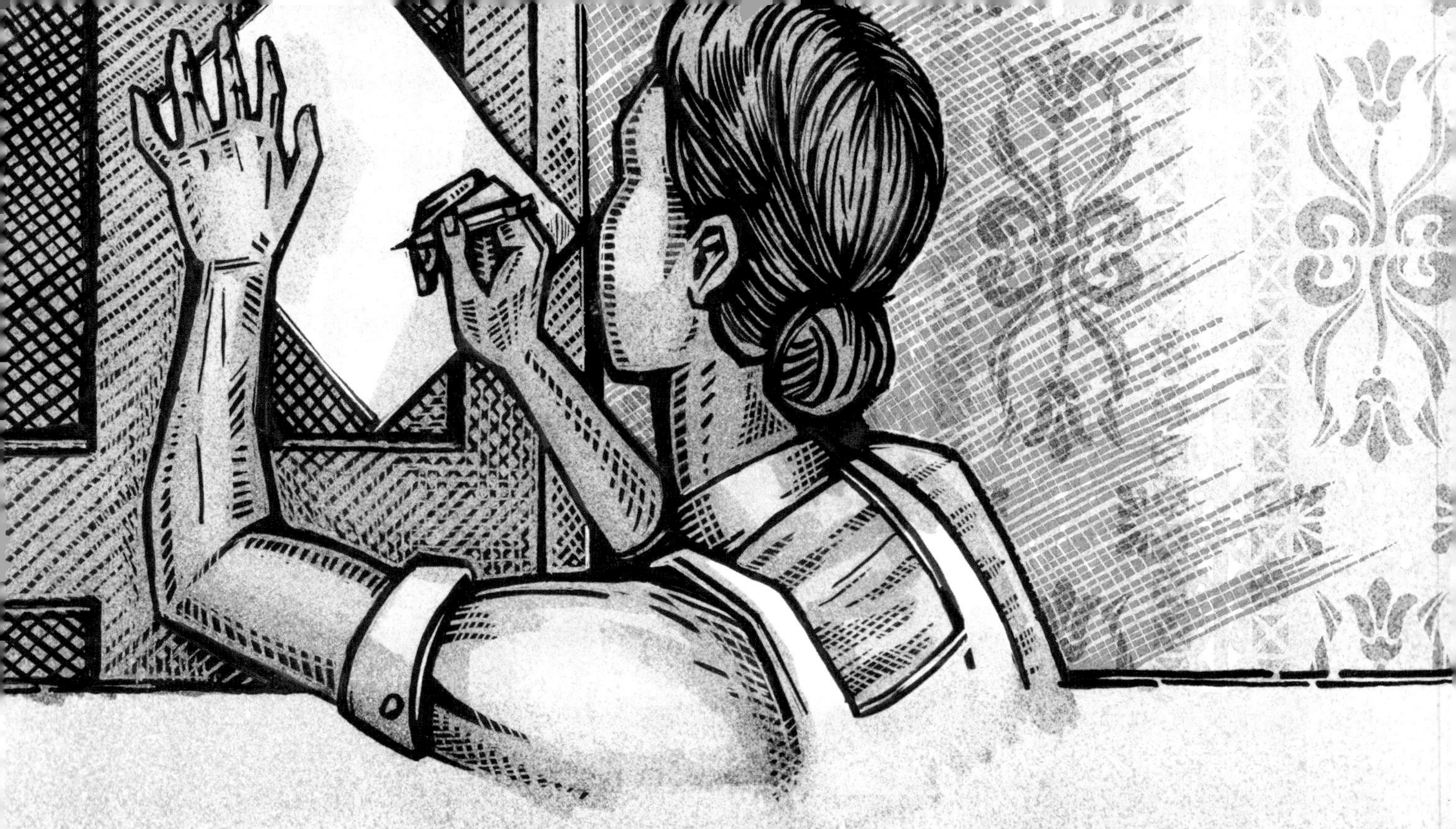

She uses the door like a table to write on. We can't move much under the bed and it's hotter than a chicken coop. The baby starts to whimper too, but that don't stop Ma. "We need a song," she says.

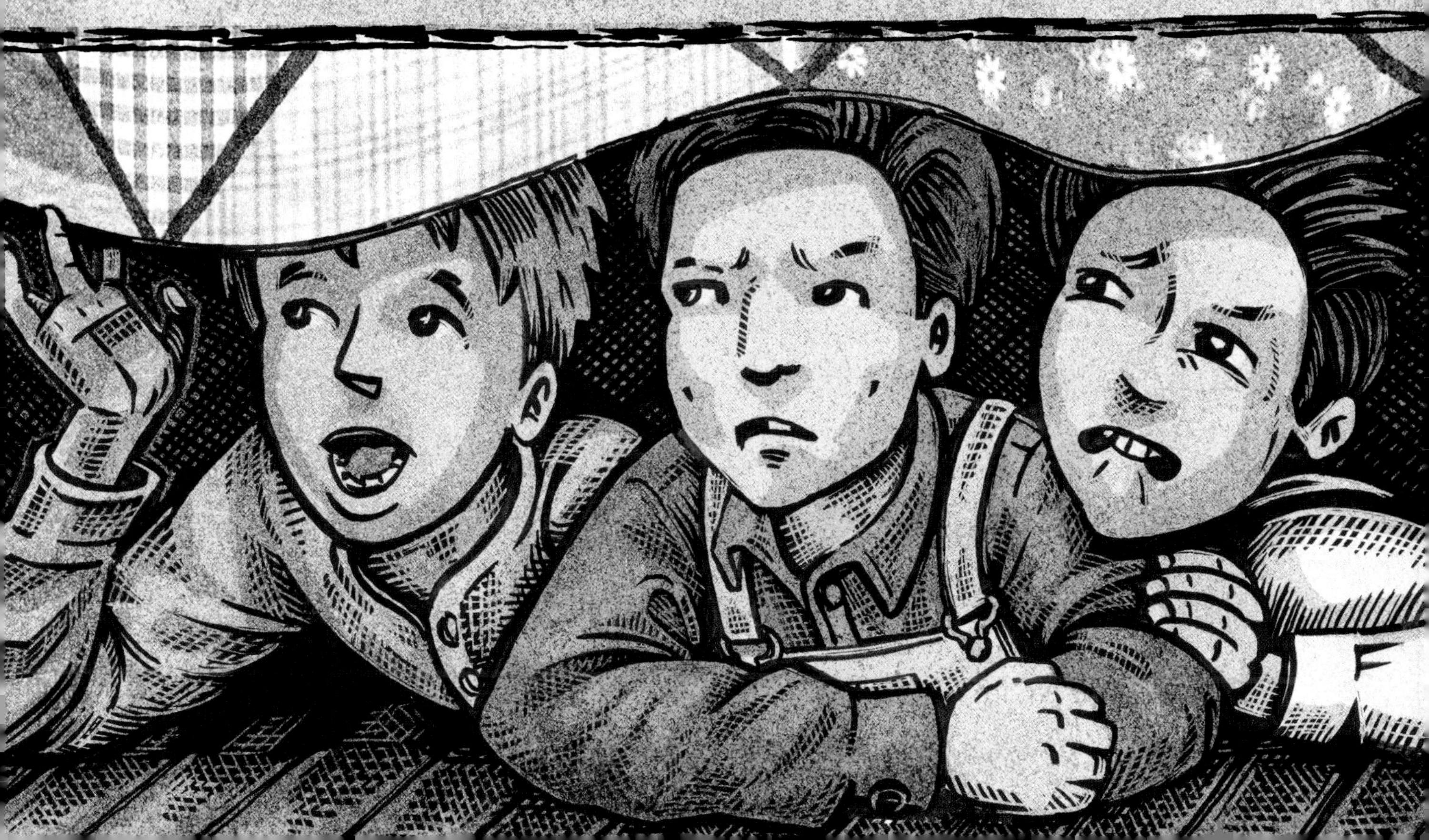

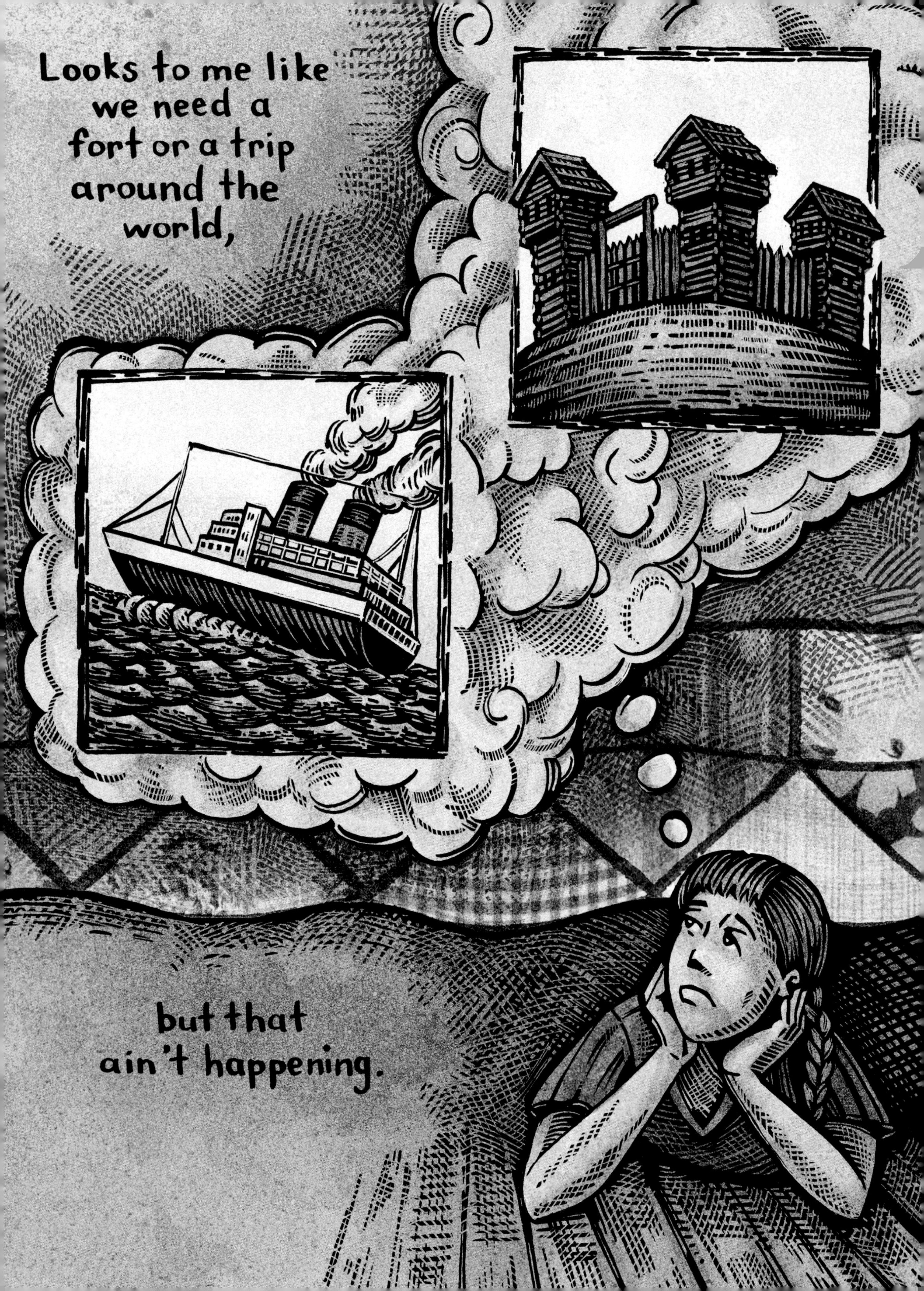
Looks to me like we need a fort or a trip around the world,
but that ain't happening.

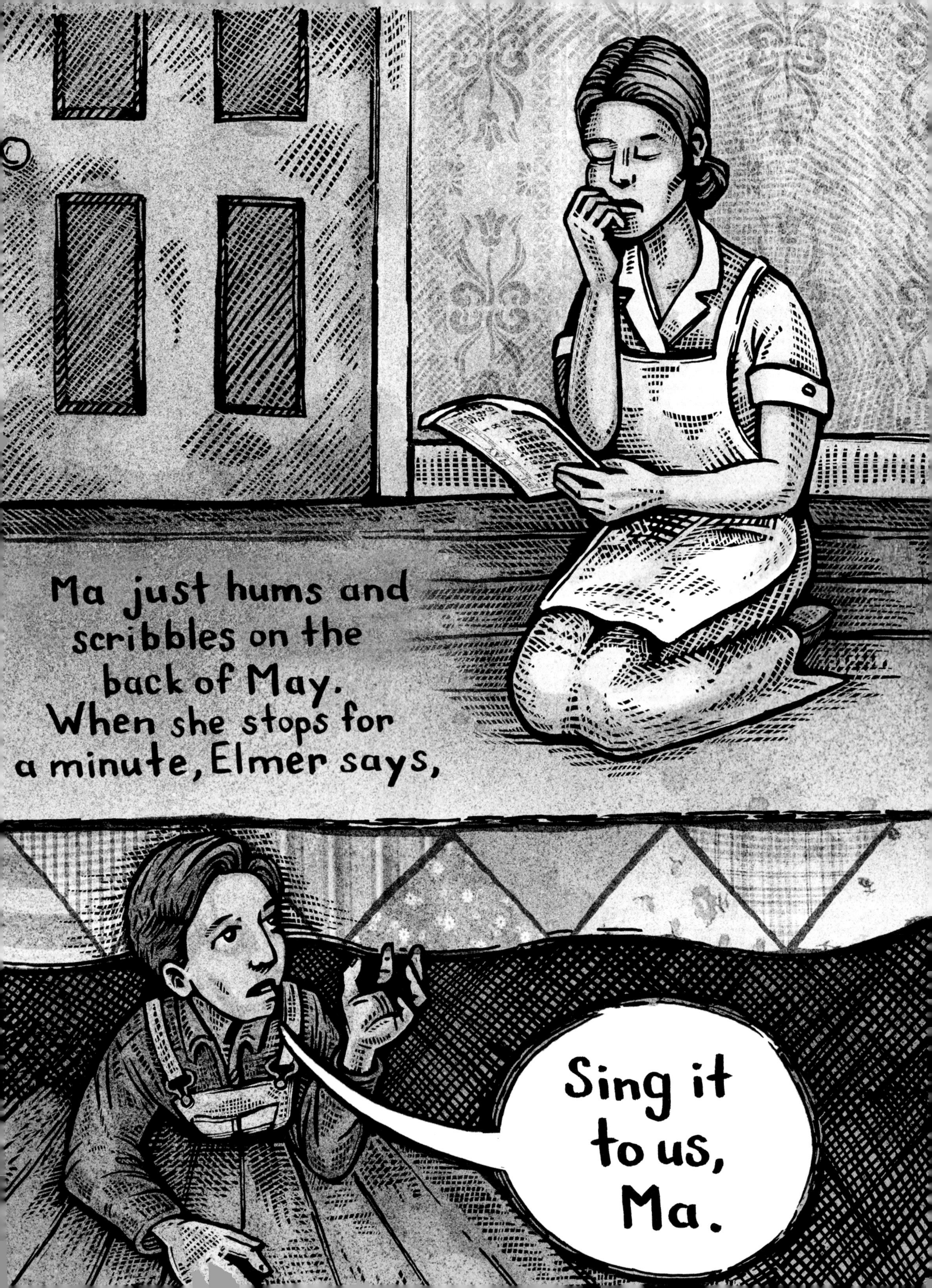
Ma just hums and scribbles on the back of May. When she stops for a minute, Elmer says,
Sing it to us, Ma.

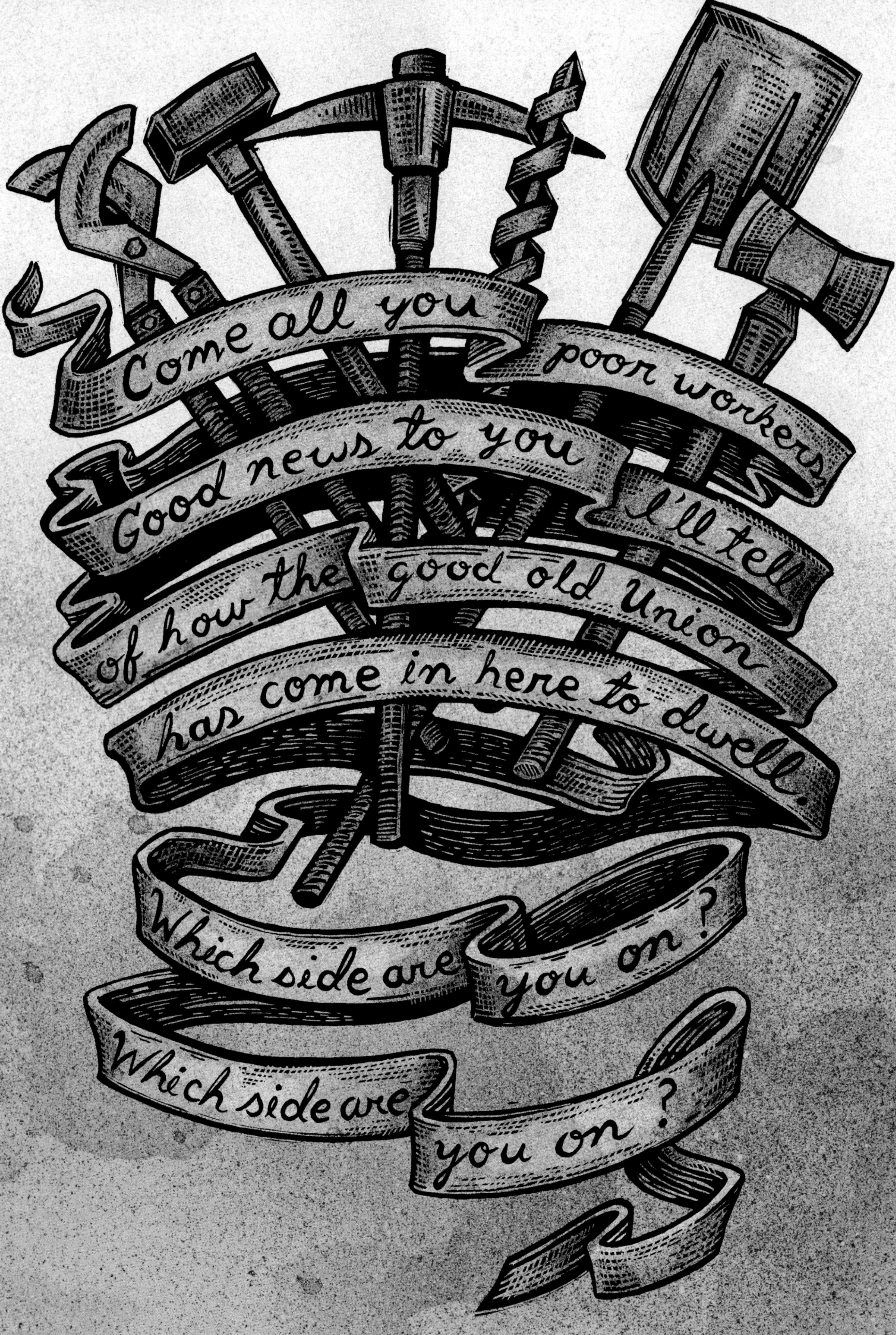
Come all you poor workers
Good news to you I'll tell
of how the good old Union
has come in here to dwell.
Which side are you on?
Which side are you on?

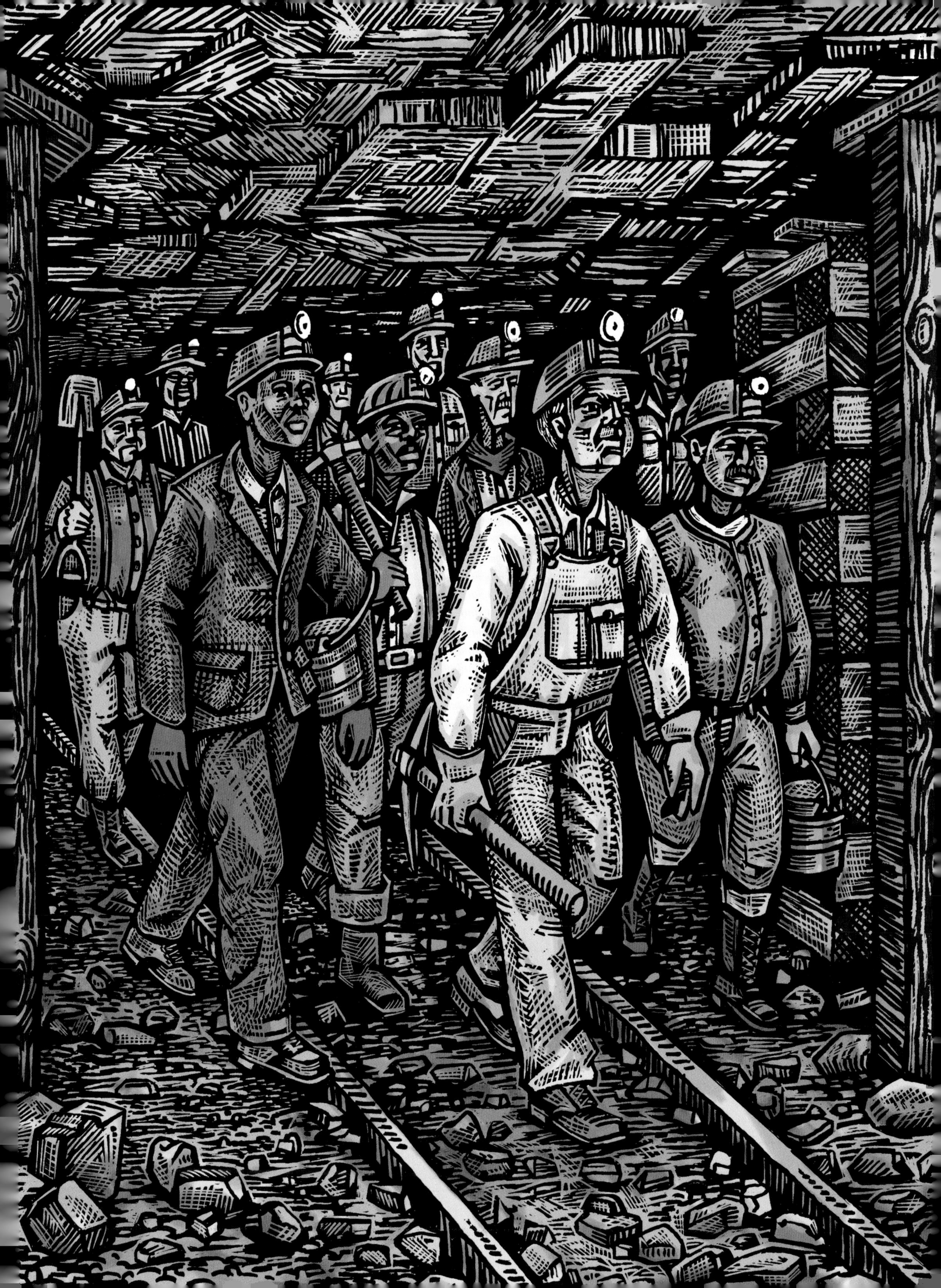

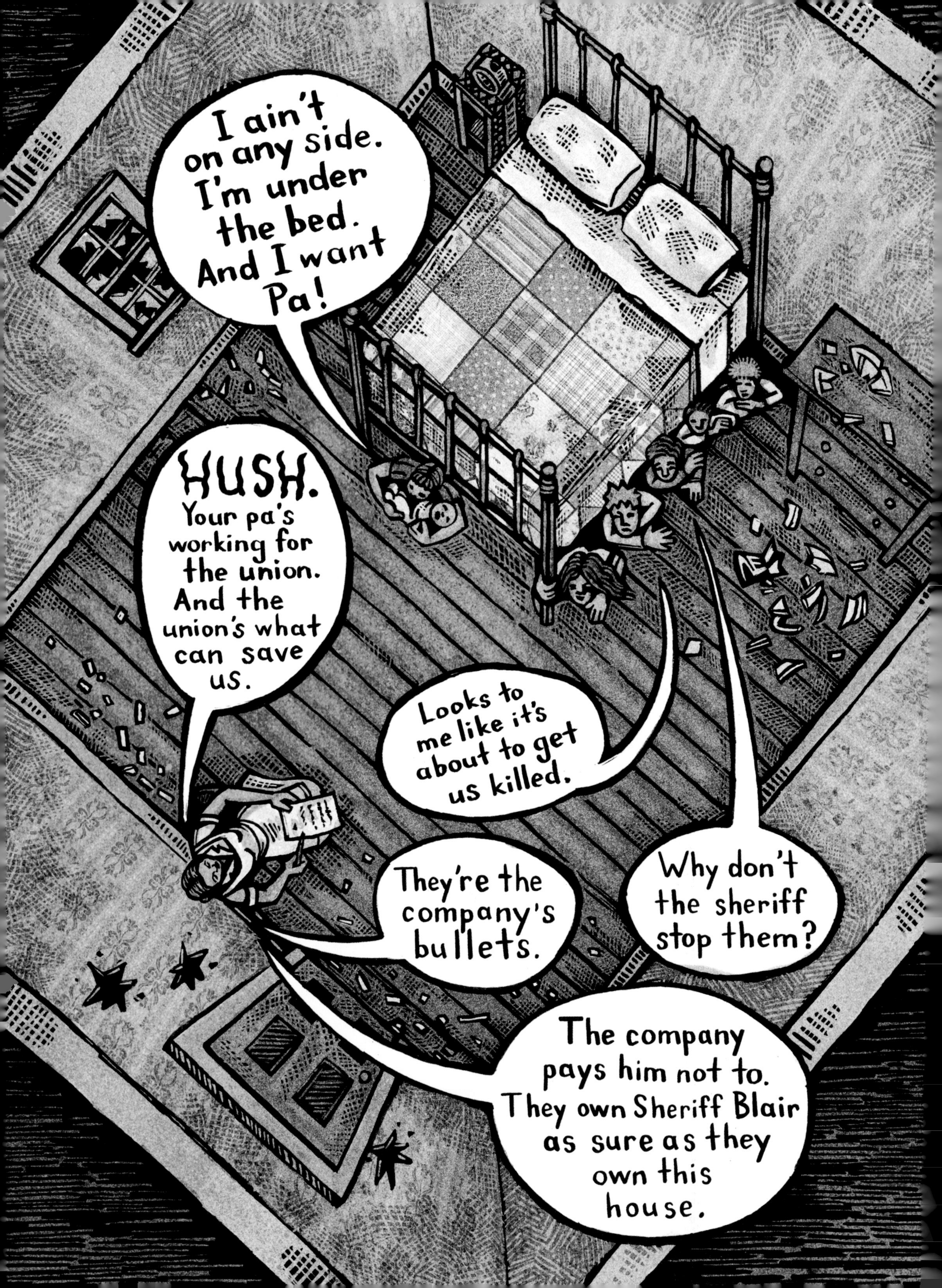
I ain't on any side. I'm under the bed. And I want Pa!
HUSH. Your pa's working for the union. And the union's what can save us.
Looks to me like it's about to get us killed.
Why don't the sheriff stop them?
They're the company's bullets.
The company pays him not to. They own Sheriff Blair as sure as they own this house.

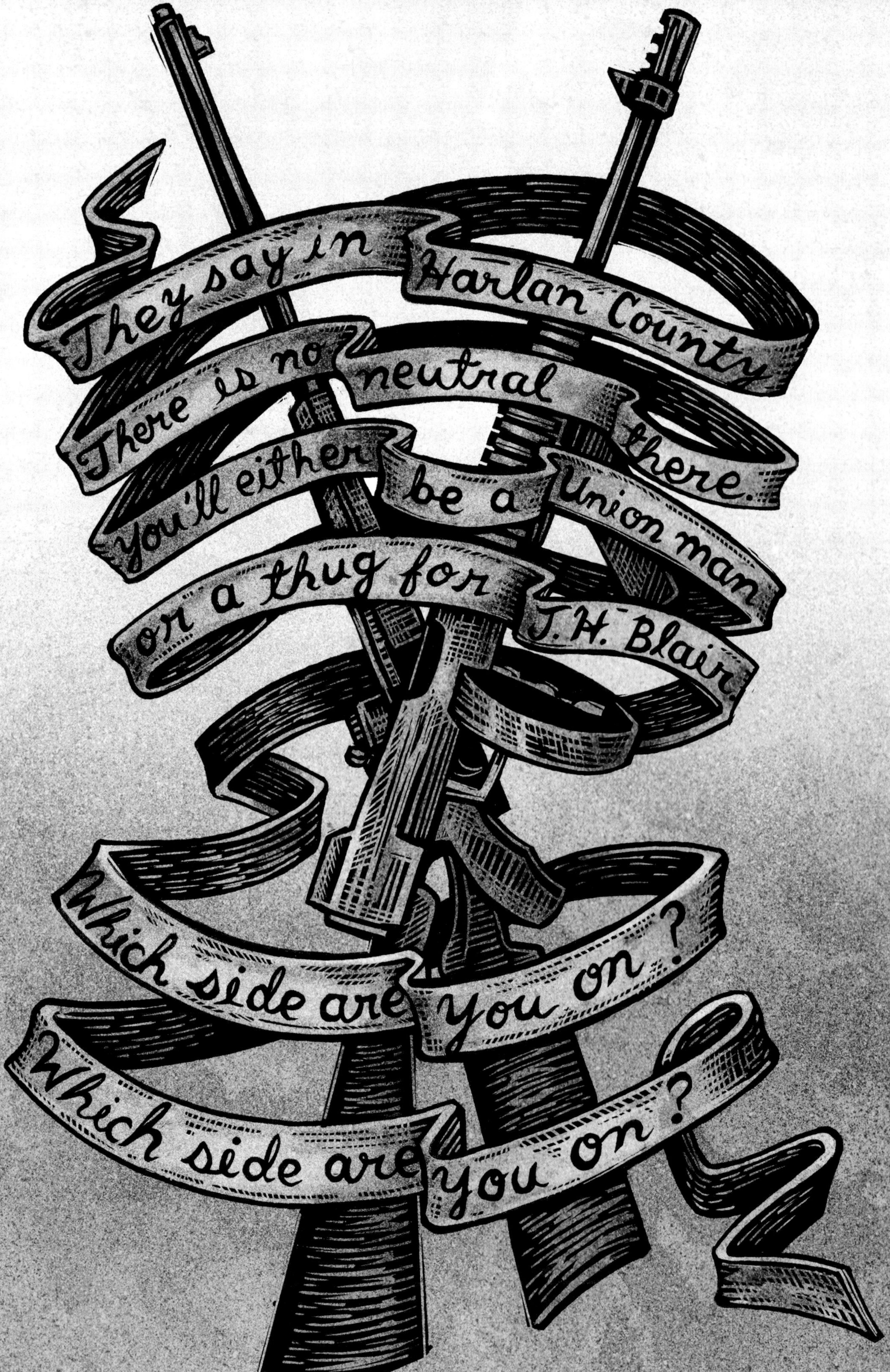
They say in Harlan County
There is no neutral there.
You'll either be a Union man
or a thug for J.H. Blair.
Which side are you on?
Which side are you on?

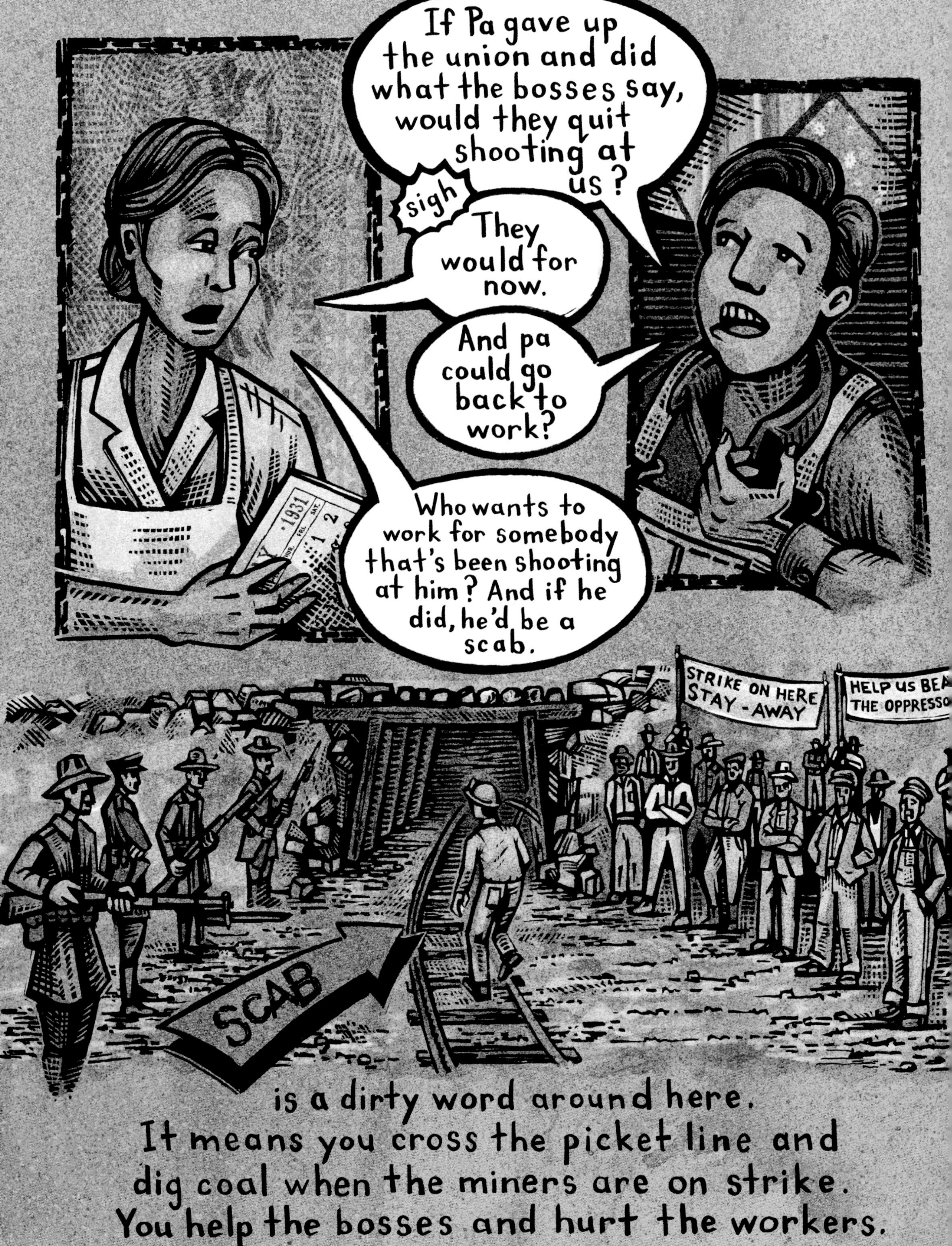
If Pa gave up the union and did what the bosses say, would they quit shooting at us?
sigh
They would for now.
And pa could go back to work?
Who wants to work for somebody that's been shooting at him? And if he did, he'd be a scab.
1931
STRIKE ON HERE STAY-AWAY
HELP US BEA THE OPPRESSO
SCAB
is a dirty word around here.
It means you cross the picket line and dig coal when the miners are on strike.
You help the bosses and hurt the workers.

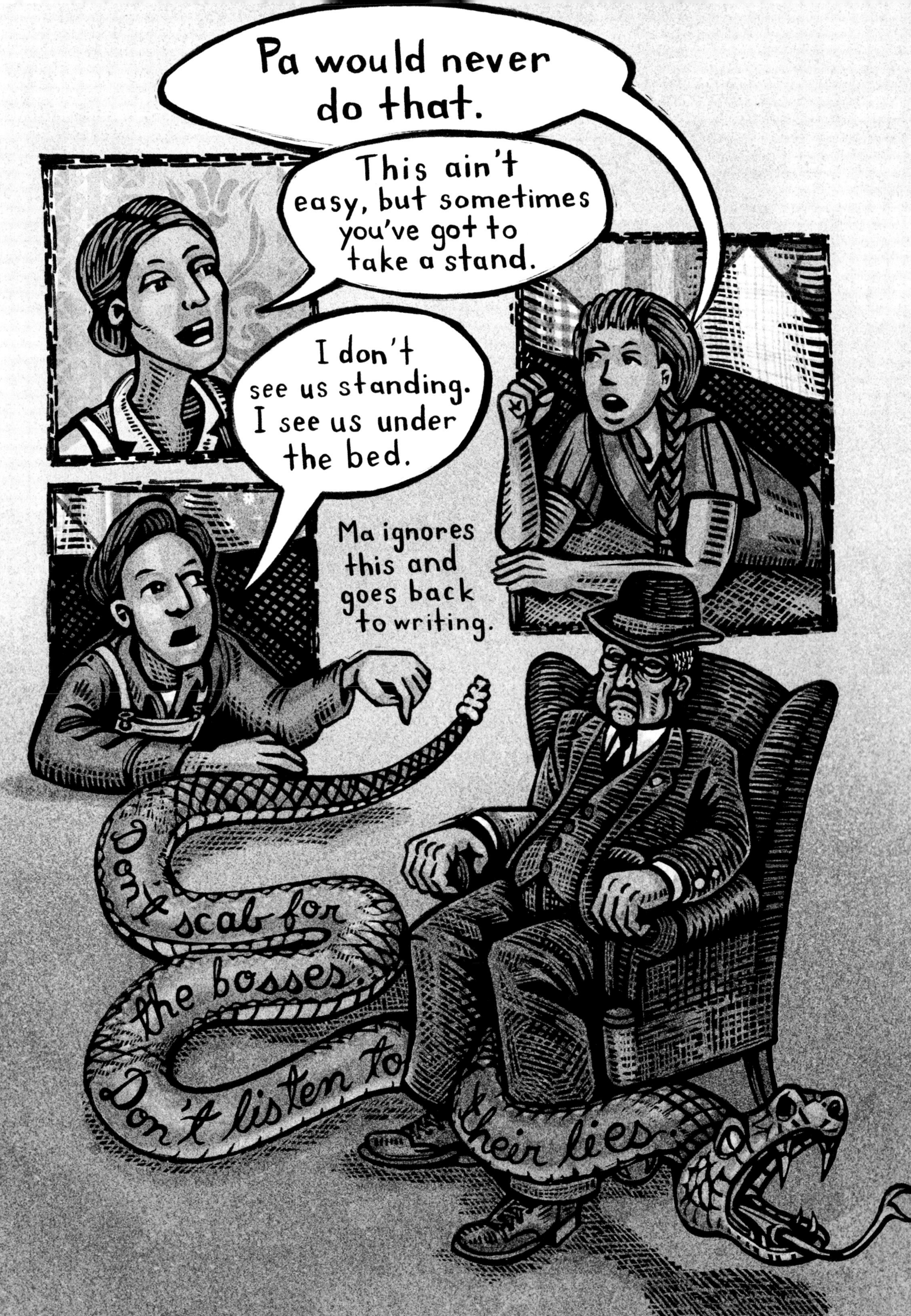
Pa would never do that.
This ain't easy, but sometimes you've got to take a stand.
I don't see us standing. I see us under the bed.
Ma ignores this and goes back to writing.
Don't scab for the bosses. Don't listen to their lies.

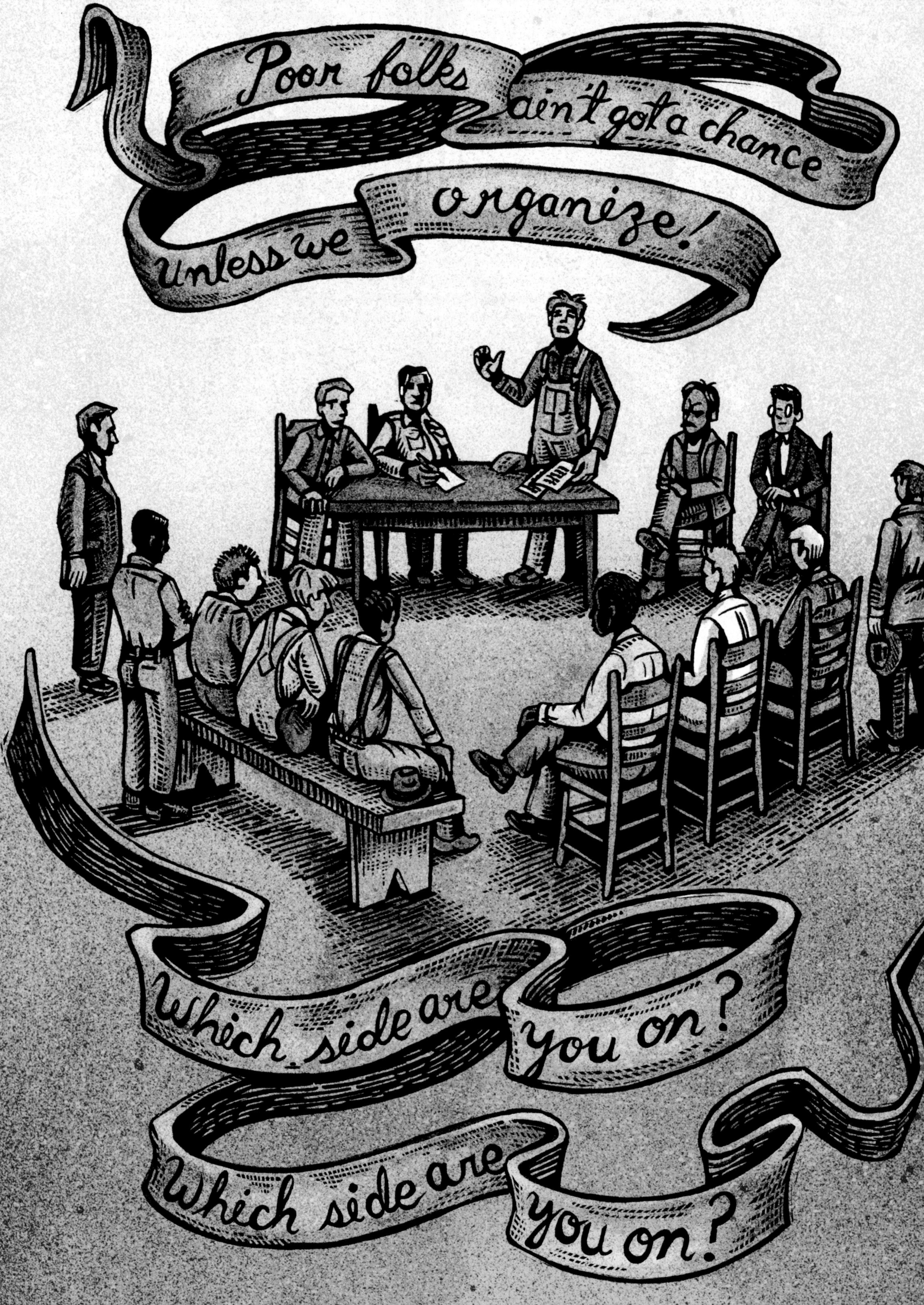
Poor folks
ain't got a chance
unless we
organize!
Which side are
you on?
Which side are
you on?

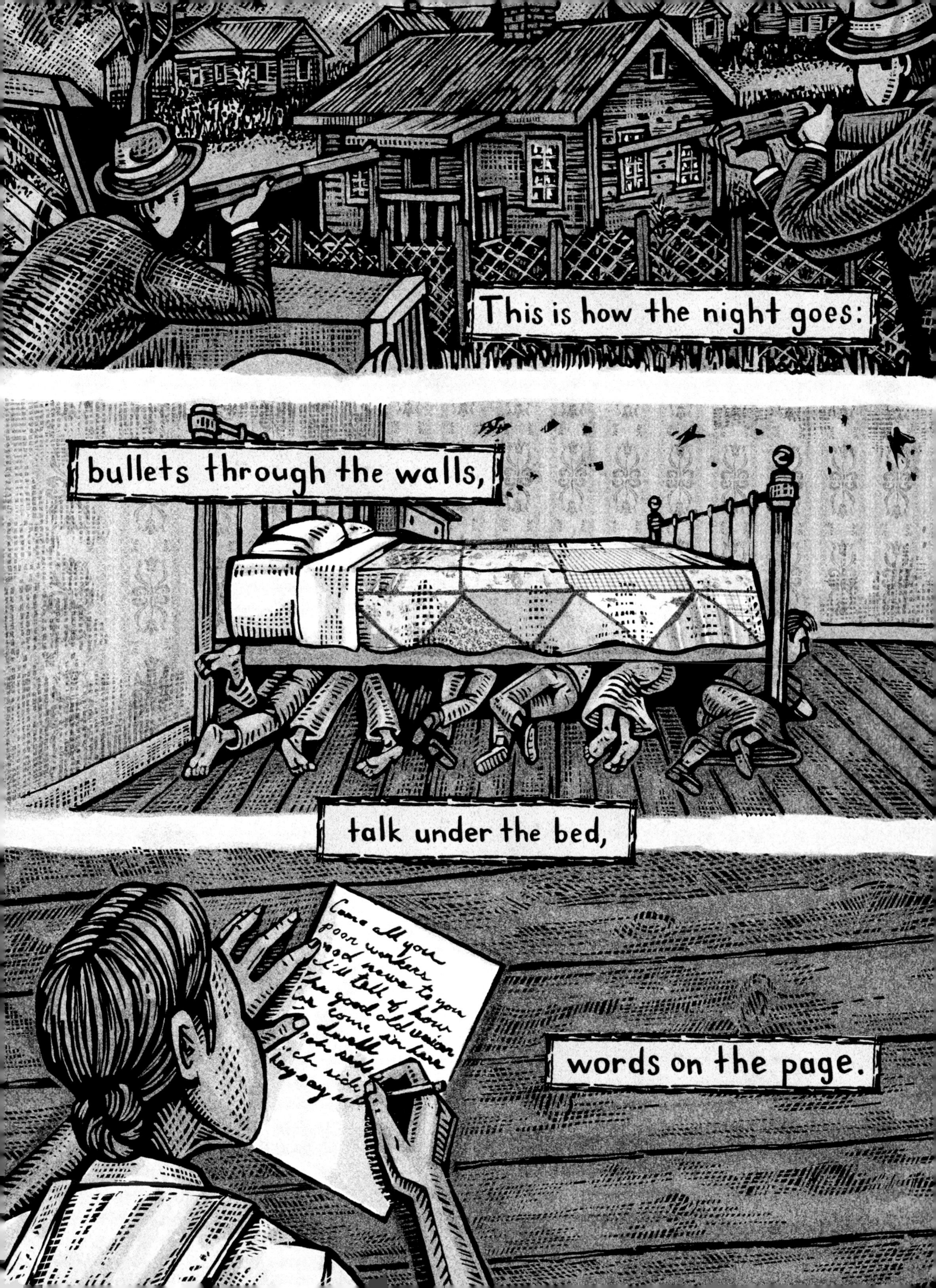

This is how the night goes:
bullets through the walls,
talk under the bed,
Come all you
poor workers
news to you
I'll tell of how
the good old union
come in here
dwell
words on the page.

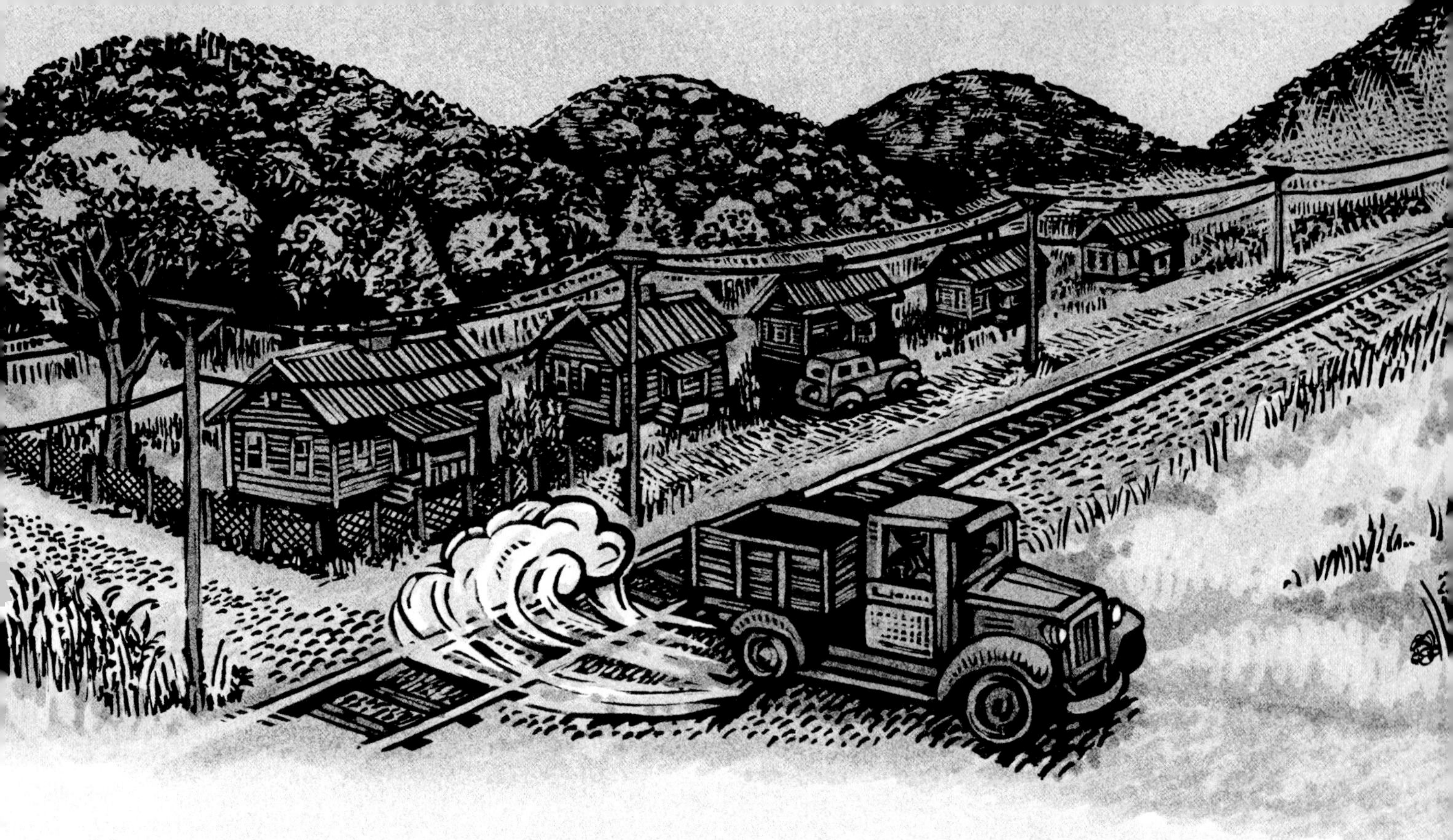

When the thugs finally quit shooting and we crawl out of hiding, we're sore and hungry, and our house is busted up, but Ma has written us a song.

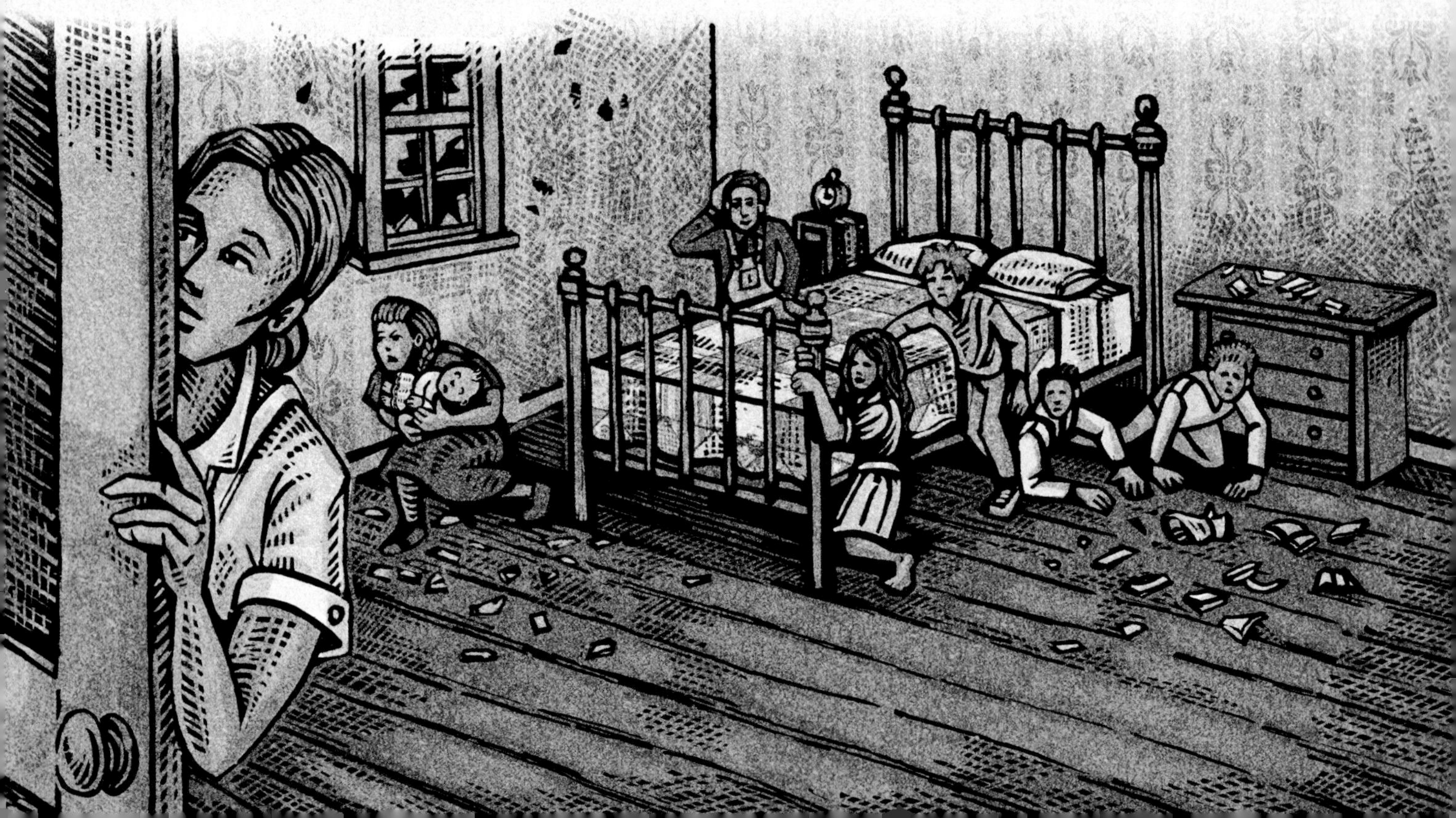

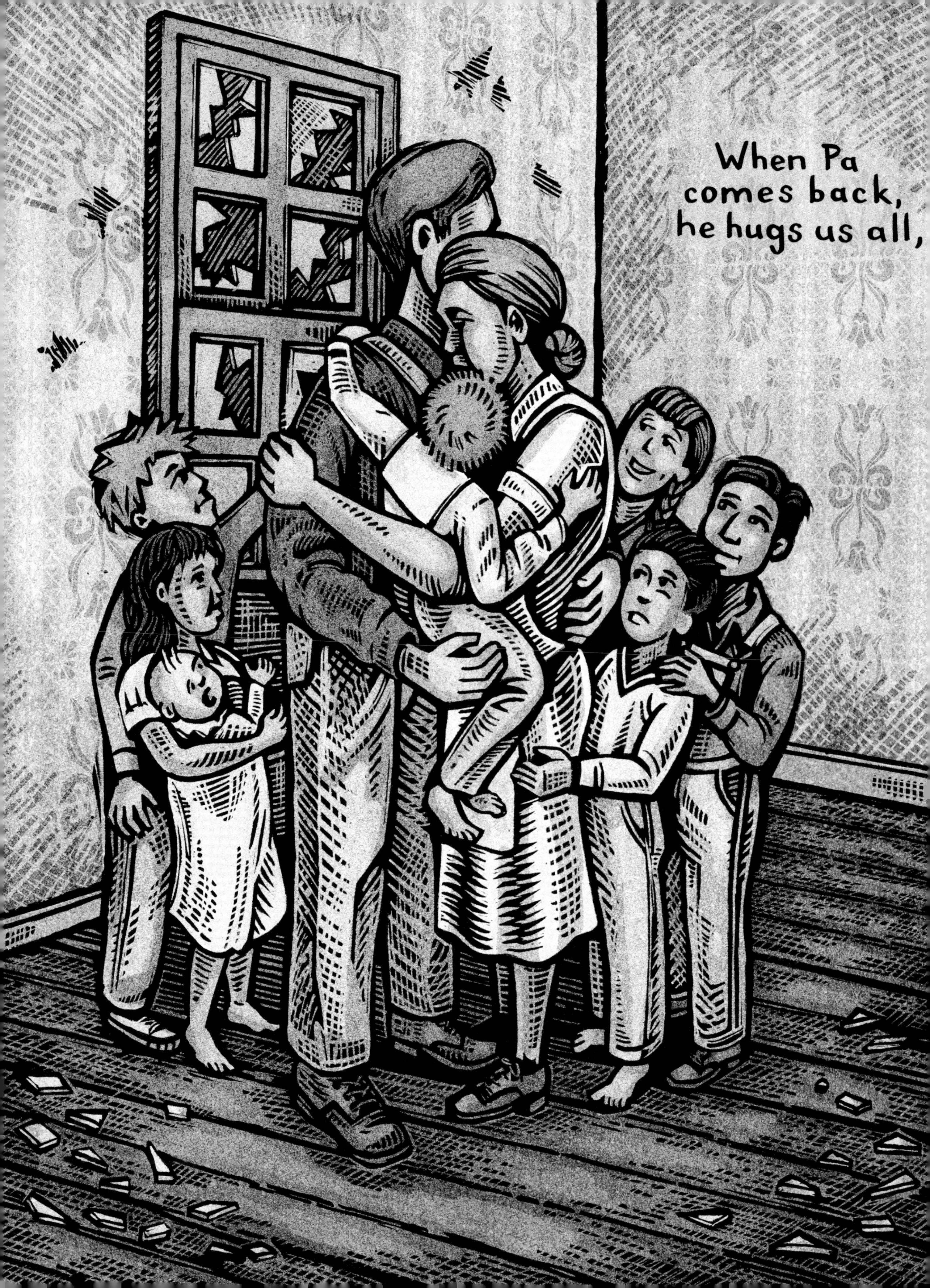

When Pa
comes back,
he hugs us all,

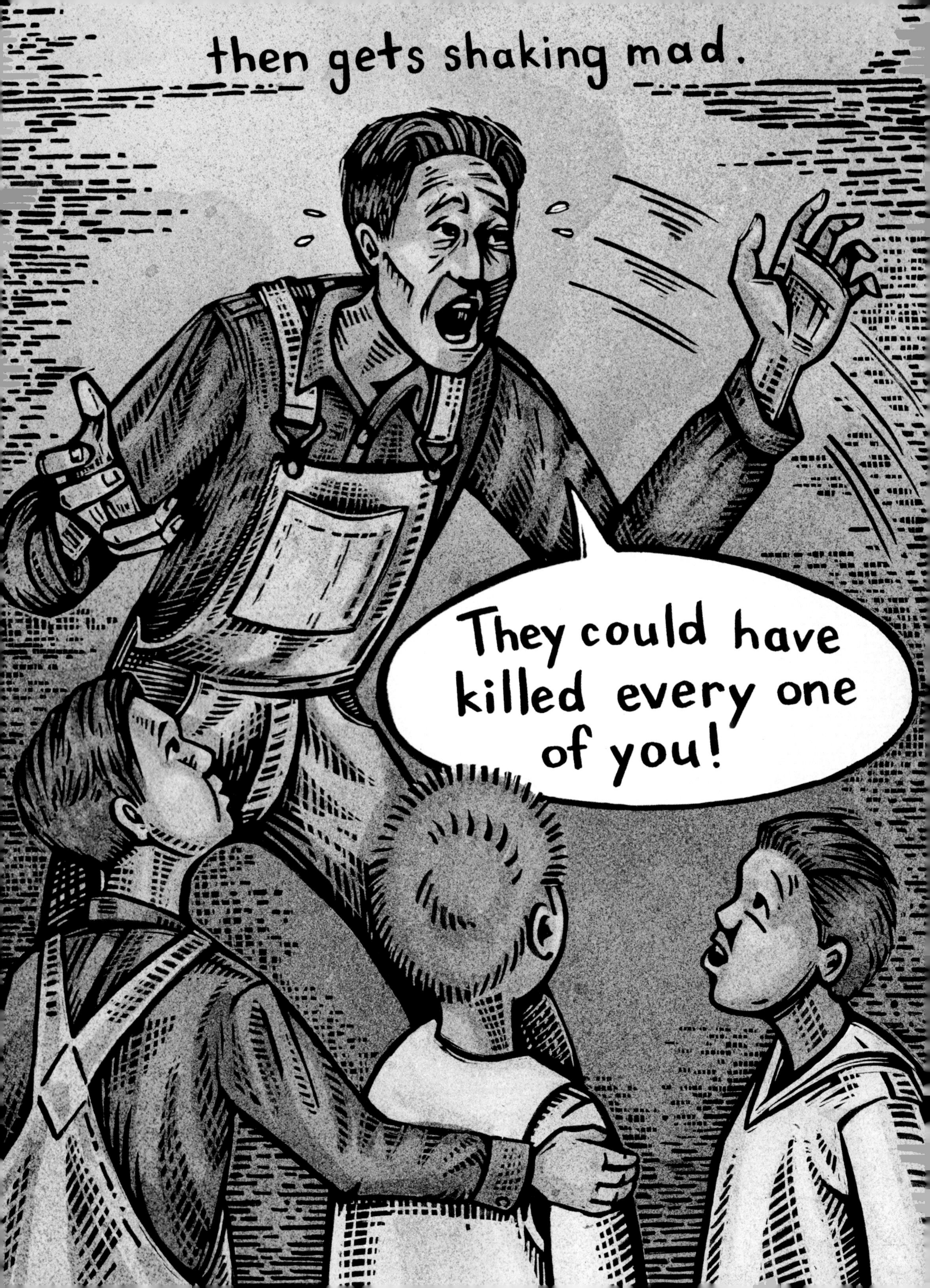
then gets shaking mad.
They could have killed every one of you!

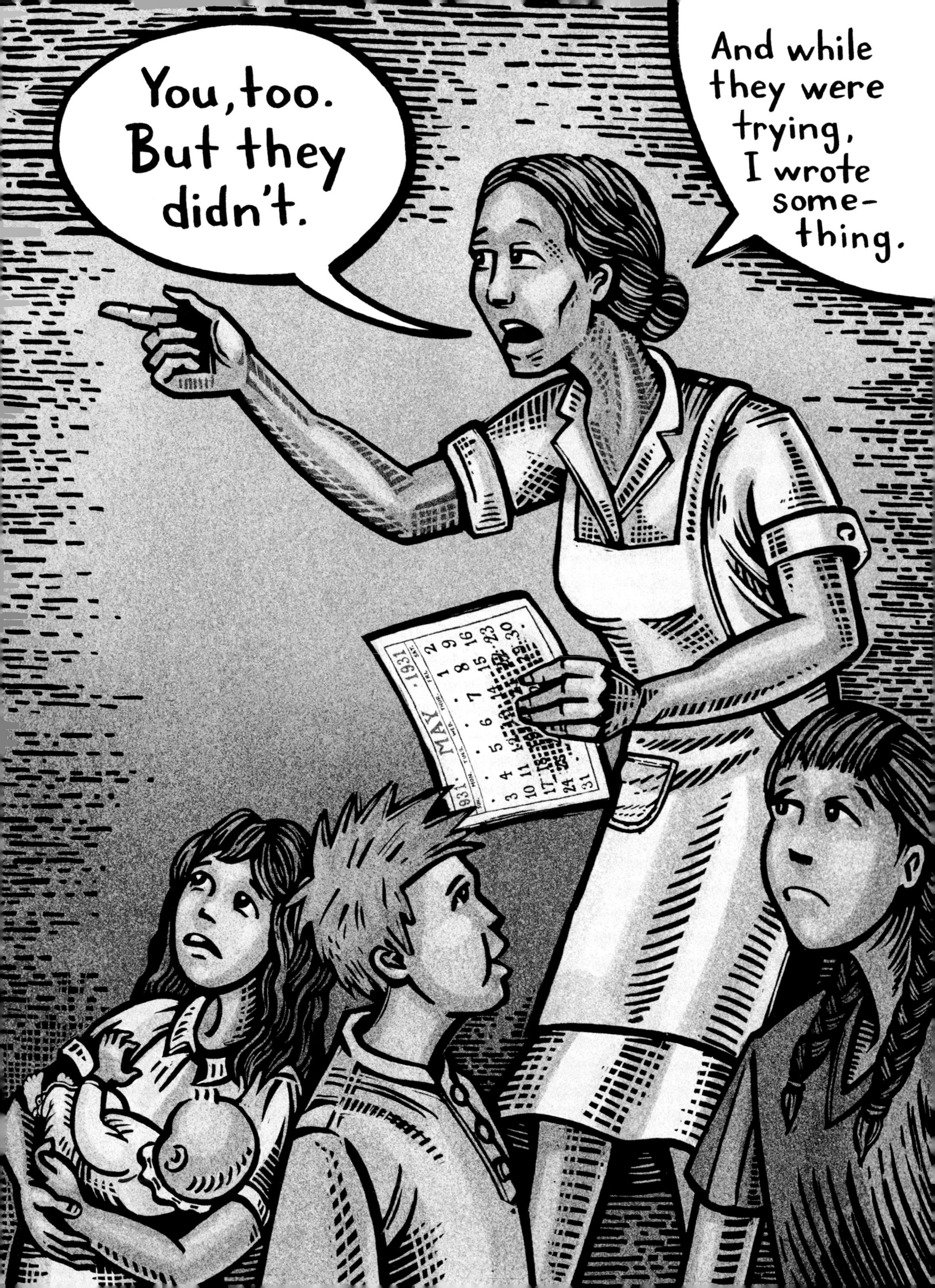
You, too. But they didn't.
And while they were trying, I wrote something.
MAY 1931

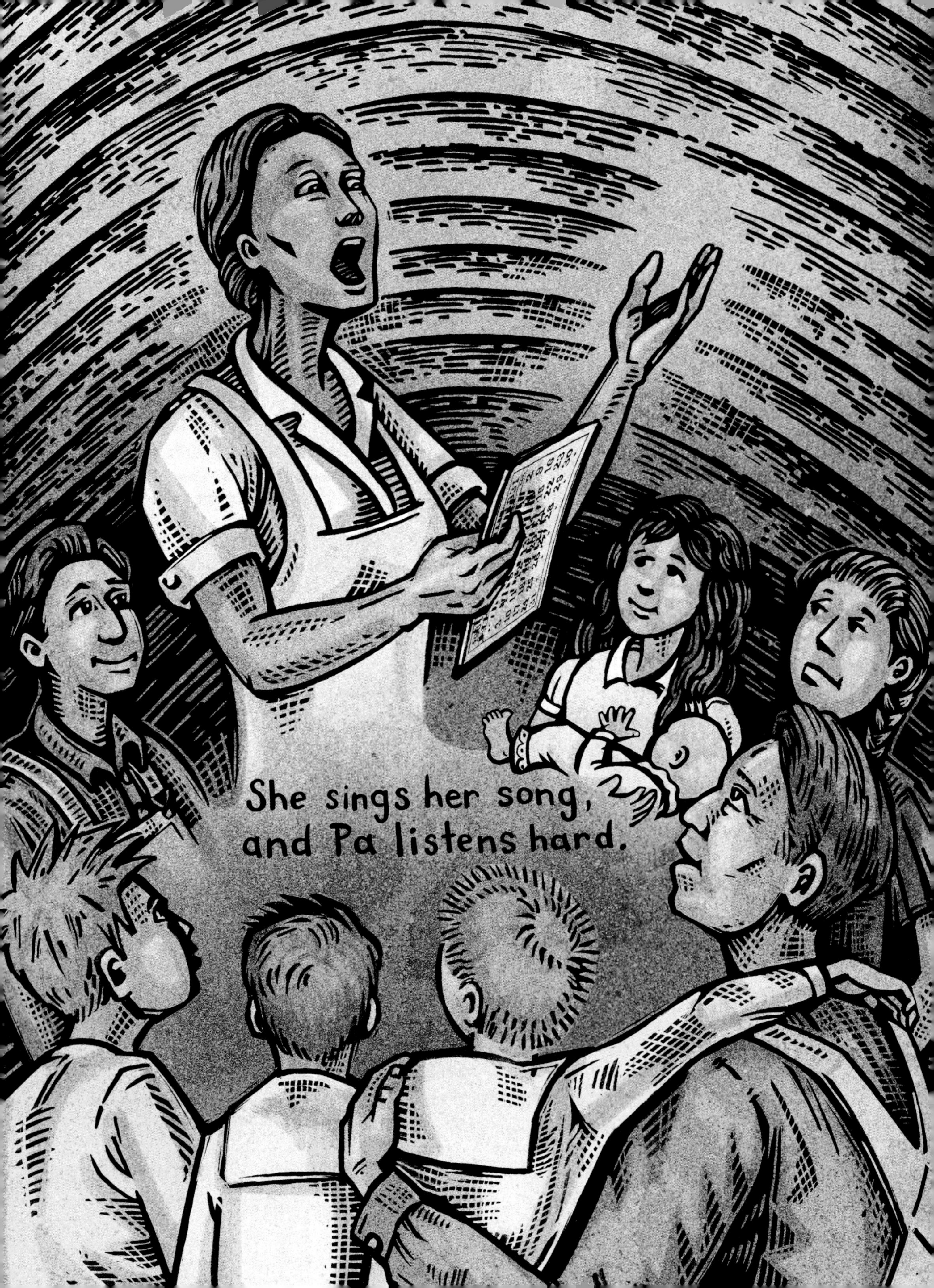

She sings her song,
and Pa listens hard.

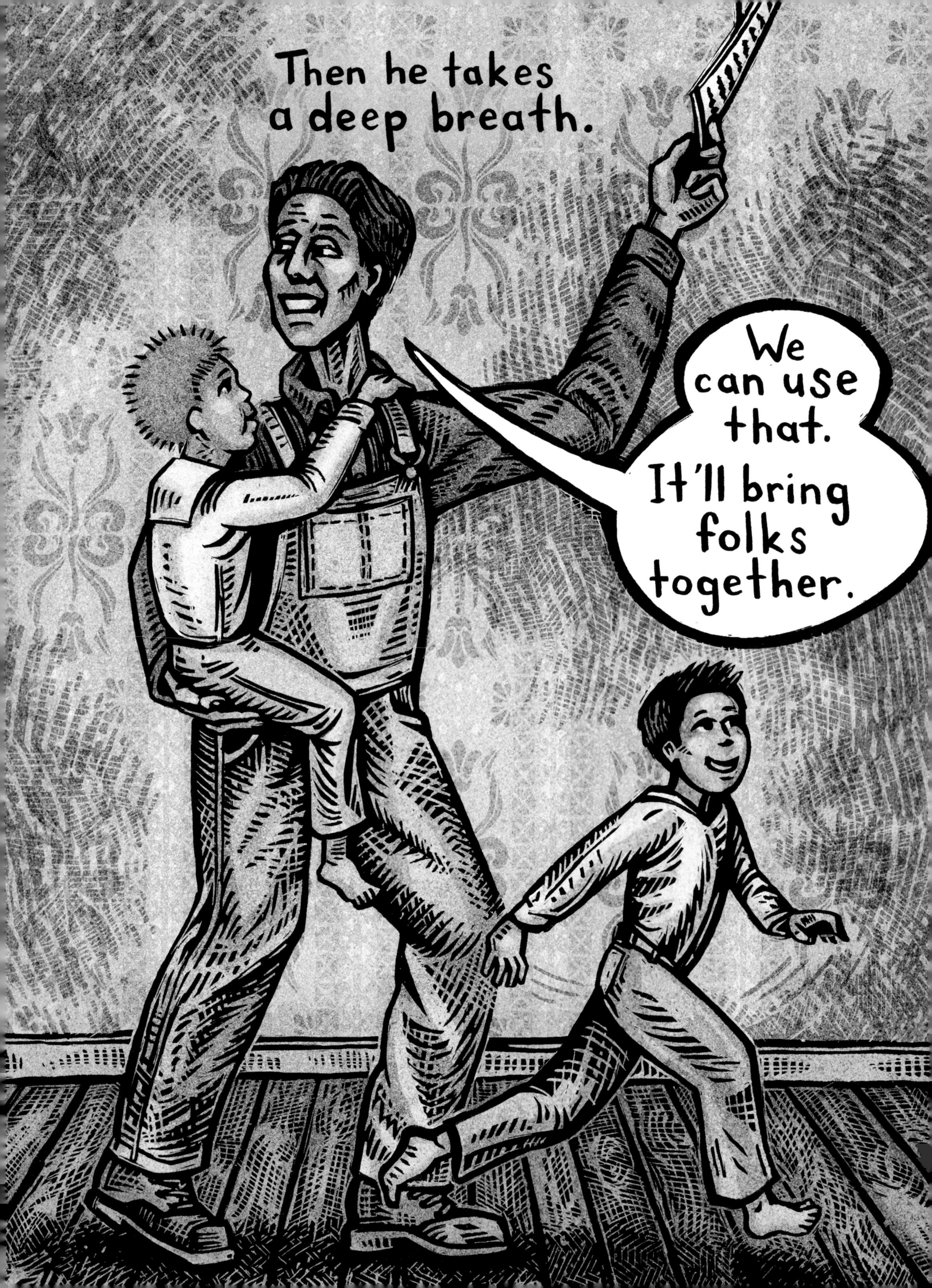
Then he takes a deep breath.
We can use that. It'll bring folks together.

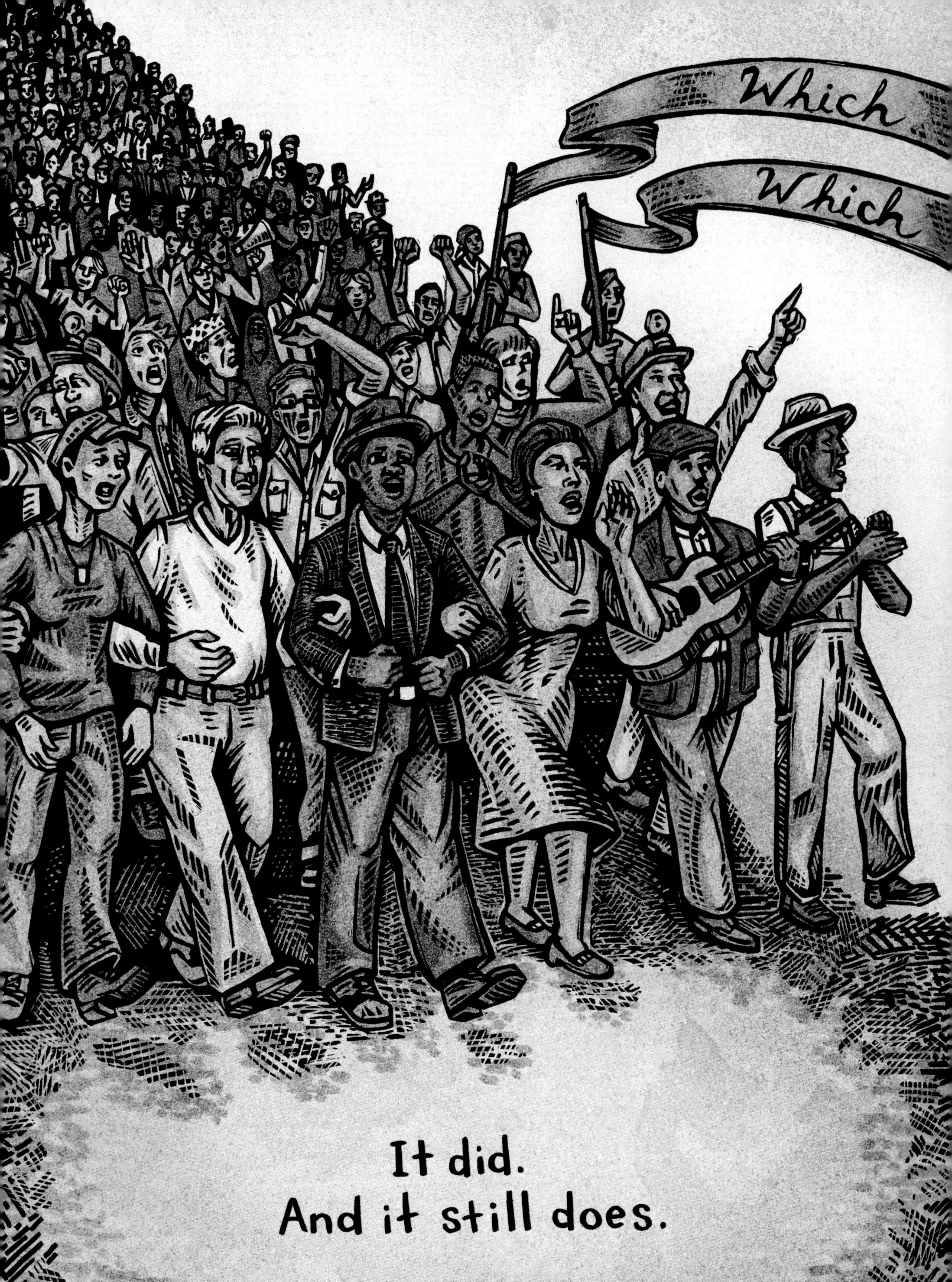
Which
Which

It did.
And it still does.

side are you on?

side are you on?

That song, written in 1931 in the mountains of Kentucky in a rain of bullets, has been sung by people fighting for their rights all over the world. And Ma, Florence Reece, lived to tell the tale.

Here she is on her 85th birthday.

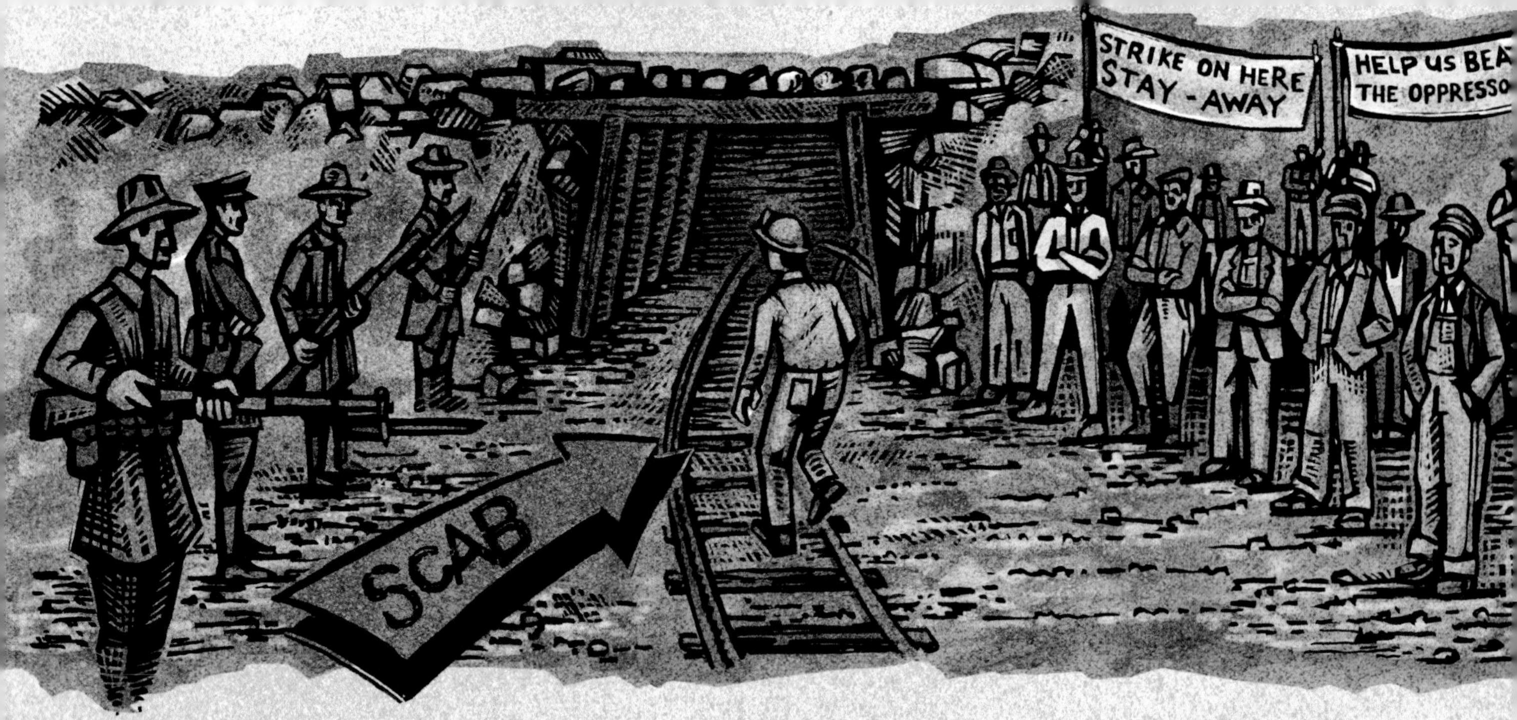
STRIKE ON HERE
STAY - AWAY
SCAB

AUTHOR'S NOTE

We human beings have a big problem with greed: wanting more than we need, more than our share. It's a lot easier to make money when you already have money, and all too often industry puts a higher value on profit than on workers' lives.

This is what was happening in the coal mines of eastern Kentucky in the 1920s and 30s. Many mines were owned by big companies far away, who didn't care what happened to miners as long as the companies got their money. Mine operators–their representatives–often kept wages low and spent as little money on safety as possible. In many cases miners weren't paid in U.S. dollars but in *scrip*, a currency good only at the commissary or company store. This system meant that prices at the store could be kept high and all a miner's earnings eventually went back to the company.

Whenever one side has all the power in a relationship something needs to change. For coal miners, change came through a series of unions–the National Miners' Union, the United Mine Workers of America–in which they banded together and went on strike (refused to work) until they got a contract giving them better pay, safer working conditions, and health care. While on strike, workers form a picket line in front of the job site and carry signs to let people know why they're not working and to warn other workers not to come take their jobs.

Changing the power structure is never easy, and that's where our story comes in. When organizers were trying to start unions in the coalfields, mine owners bribed county officials, including those enforcing the law, to try to stop them. They brought in outside workers, called scabs, to cross the picket line and keep the coal mines going. When strikers couldn't stop the flow of coal, they lost the workers' one power: to withhold their labor and stop production. Violence broke out on both sides.

Deputies and hired killers (gun thugs) attacked organizers and their families. Strikers fought back and sometimes attacked scabs. This violence gave Harlan County, Kentucky–where I'm from–its other name: Bloody Harlan.

Sam Reece, Florence's husband, was a union organizer, and Sheriff Blair's deputies were after him. They attacked the Reece house more than once, and it was during the worst of those assaults that Florence wrote "Which Side Are You On?". In the folk tradition, she used a tune she already knew and made up new words for it. Some say it was a hymn, "Lay the Lily Low"; others say it was the ballad "Jack Munro." A lot of great songs were born this way. You might try it yourself.

We don't know where "Which Side Are You On?" was first sung, but it's gone around the world in the eighty years since. If you go to YouTube you can watch many versions today.

As often happens with folk songs, singers have changed and added verses as needed, and one of the most famous verses–the one that ends, "Poor folks ain't got a chance / Unless we organize"–doesn't appear in Reece's published version. I include it here because it's a rallying cry, and anyone who knows the song would miss it.

That's one of the great qualities of folk songs. They may have one originator, like Reece for "Which Side," but they have many makers. Folk songs are alive. Singers add their strengths and causes and make their own versions.

Stories are like this too. You can find many accounts of how Florence Reece wrote the song and they won't all agree. (You'd probably discover the same thing if you asked everybody in your family to give their account of one event. We remember things differently. And what we remember changes.)

My version of this story comes from Bev Futrell, a member of The Reel World String Band, who heard it from Reece herself at the Highlander Education Center on the occasion of Reece's 85th birthday celebration. For many years, Florence and Sam Reece were affiliated with that famous social justice training center in Tennessee, where people such as Martin Luther King Jr., Rosa Parks, and Pete Seeger came together to plan ways to make our society more just.

Like anything we humans make, unions are not perfect. Greed for money and power takes hold in unions too. But there is no denying the positive role of unions in improving working conditions and establishing workers' rights.

All these issues are very much alive today, when wealth and power are held by a small percentage of people so that the gap between rich and poor continues to widen. Look around and see what you can find about social justice where you are. It's never too soon to become informed, decide what you think, and speak out. You have a choice. You have a voice. We are how change happens.

BIBLIOGRAPHY

Primary:
- Beverly Futrell, introduction for "Which Side Are You On?" The Reel World String Band concert, Lexington Public Library, June 5, 2004.
- Interviews with Fran Ansley, Brenda Bell, Bill Murrah, and June Rosten, all of whom knew Florence and Sam Reece.
- Florence Reece, *Against the Current: Poems and Stories* (Keith Press: Knoxville, Tn., 1981).
- Florence Reece talks about and sings part of "Which Side Are You On?" at http://www.youtube.com/watch?v=WYr09q9dHSo
  You can hear her sing the whole song at http://www.youtube.com/watch?v=Nzudto-FA5Y&NR=1
  Online, you can also listen to versions by Natalie Merchant, Pete Seeger, and many others. Words will vary, as people shape the song to fit their tongues and occasions. *This is the folk process!*
- Video interviews with Florence Reece, Coal Employment Project Records Collection, Tapes 119 and 140, East Tennessee State University, Johnson City, Tennessee.
- "Appalachian Workshop: Discussion of the Appalachian Region by Florence Reece, George Tucker, and Others," Highlander Center, New Market, Tennessee. 1973. From the Broadside Collection, East Tennessee State.
- "Which Side Are You On? An Interview with Florence Reece," *Mountain Life and Work*, 48 (March 1942), 22–4.

Secondary:
- Fran Ansley, Brenda Bell, and Florence Reece, interviewers. "'Little David Blues:' An interview with Tom Lowry." *Southern Exposure*, vol. 1, Nos. 3 & 4.
- *Harlan County, U.S.A.* Barbara Kopple, producer and director. Academy Award for Best Documentary, 1976. (Florence Reece appears in this film.)
- *Labor Notes* http://www.labornotes.org/node/1385
- Loyal Jones, review of *Against the Current. Appalachian Journal*, Fall 1984.
- Alessandro Portelli, *They Say in Harlan County: An Oral History*. Oxford University Press, 2010.

Further Reading:
For more on Appalachian children's books, including many that feature coal mining, see the indispensable:
- Roberta Teague Herrin and Sheila Quinn Oliver, *Appalachian Children's Literature: An Annotated Bibliography*, Macfarland, 2010.
- Tina Hanlon, et. al. *Resources for Readers and Teachers of Appalachian Literature*. www.applit.org

ACKNOWLEDGMENTS

In addition to those noted in the Bibliography, the author wishes to thank the following people whose help was vital to this book:

- Karen Reece Cox, Florence Reece's granddaughter, who read the text and shared her memories.
- Highlander Research and Educational Foundation, especially Susan Williams, Pam McMichaels, and Candie Carawan.
- Roberta Herrin, Director of the Center for Appalachian Studies at East Tennessee State University.
- Richard Jackson, who liked it from the beginning.
- Gary Hamilton, who took the photograph of Florence Reece.
- Charlotte Nolan: actress, writer, teacher, and life-long friend.
- Rose Cohelia, who facilitated our visit to the Clover Fork Coal Company.
- Larry Lafollette, Director of Archives, Southeast Community and Technical College, Cumberland, Kentucky.
- Ned Irwin, University Archivist, East Tennessee State University.

The illustrator wishes to thank:

- Lewis Holman, who put me in touch with Charlotte Nolan, his close family friend in Harlan, Kentucky.
- Charlotte Nolan, Rose Cohelia, and her daughter Katharine, for welcoming me to Harlan and going out of their way to show me their hometown. Their help was an invaluable aide in the visual research for this book.
- Sharon, Macéo, Anthony, Bob, P.J., Ricardo and Colin–my family and friends who helped and supported me every step of the way.
- Eric, Melissa, and Lauren for helping me achieve my goals on a weekly basis.
- James Couch for being a good neighbor at the campsite in Kingdom Come State Park, Cumberland, Kentucky.
- Zefrey, Scott, and Christian.

The author and illustrator wish to thank:

- The Appalachian Studies Center at Eastern Tennessee State University–Pat Gerard, student archivist; John Fleenor, photo and music archivist; and Amy Collins, Interim Director.
- Kentucky Coal Mining Museum in Benham–Phyllis Sizemore, Director; Mike Obradovich, tour guide and retired miner.
- Carl W. Buck Shoupe, retired miner from Lynch, Kentucky, and Rodney S. Adams, retired miner from Benham, Kentucky.
- Marie Whitfield, who took us on a tour of the offices and company store of Clover Fork Coal Company, which closed in 1957.
- Bryan W. Whitfield Jr. Public Library in Harlan, Kentucky.
- The Edsel T. Godbey Appalachian Center at Southeast Kentucky Community and Technical College.

For information, write Cinco Puntos Press, 701 Texas, El Paso, TX 79901 or call at (915) 838-1625.
Printed in the United States by Worzalla.
First Edition
10 9 8 7 6 5 4 3 2 1

Library of Congress Cataloging-in-Publication Data
Lyon, George Ella, 1949-
Which side are you on? : the story of a song / by George Ella Lyon ; illustrated by Christopher Cardinale. – 1st ed.
p. cm.
ISBN 978-1-933693-96-5 (alk. paper)
1. Reece, Florence, 1900-1986. Which side are you on?—Juvenile literature. 2. Miners—Kentucky—Songs and music—History and criticism—Juvenile literature. 3. Miners—Labor unions—Kentucky—Songs and music—Juvenile literature. I. Cardinale, Christopher, ill. II. Title.
ML3930.R323L96 2011
782.42'1592—dc22
2010037398

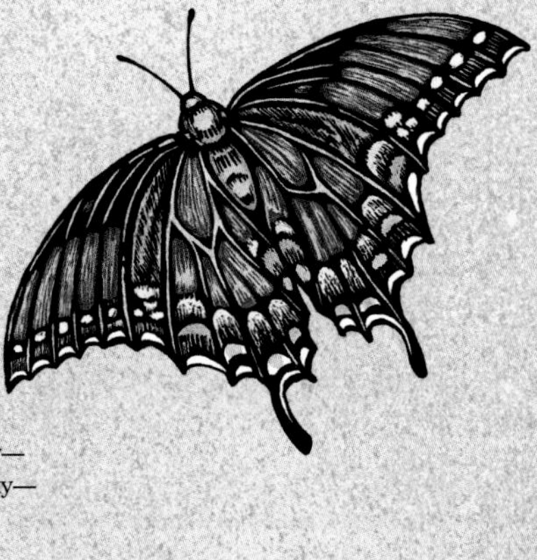

Special thanks to Sharon Kwik for her generous work masking and compositing the final artwork.

Book design by Anne M. Giangiulio